sing a song *of* poetry

A Teaching Resource for Phonics, Word Study, and Fluency

fold here

1. Make one copy of the poem as a master.

2. Fold the Suggestions up out of sight before making copies for your children.

3. Make copies for children to use in class or share with their families.

This reproducible, one-per-page format enables you to share (when appropriate) printed copies of the poems with your children after you've worked with and enjoyed the poems together in class.

FirstHand
An imprint of Heinemann
A division of Reed Elsevier Inc.
361 Hanover Street
Portsmouth, NH 03801–3912
www.firsthand.heinemann.com

Offices and agents throughout the world

© 2004 by Gay Su Pinnell and Irene C. Fountas

Library of Congress Cataloging-in-Publication Data

CIP data is on file with the Library of Congress.

ISBN 0-325-00657-1

Printed in the United States of America on acid-free paper

07 06   ML   3 4 5 6

Sing a Song of Poetry

A Teaching Resource for Phonics, Word Study, and Fluency

Introduction

Sing a Song of Poetry rolls off the tongue and moves the heart and spirit, if not the feet and hands. Rhythmical language of any sort delights young children as it surrounds them with the magical sounds of dancing words. But poetry, verse, and song provide the magic of teaching as well; indeed, oral language is the doorway to the world of written language and the foundation for literacy. As second graders respond to the sound patterns, intriguing words, and inspiring ideas they find in poems, songs, and rhymes, they are learning invaluable lessons about the ways in which our language works – knowledge that will serve them well as they become readers and writers.

The poems, songs, and rhymes in this volume are a rich source of language, ideas, and imagery that will help second graders use and enjoy oral and written language. This volume is a companion to the lessons described in *Phonics Lessons, Grade 2: Letters, Words, and How They Work* (Pinnell and Fountas 2003, Heinemann). It can also be used as a stand-alone resource for language and literacy opportunities in any primary classroom.

Experiences with poetry help children become aware of the phonological system of language and provide a foundation for matching sounds with letters, letter clusters, and word parts. You can use poems, chants, and songs to help children:

▶ Listen for and identify rhyming words.

▶ Identify words with the same beginning, ending, or medial sound.

▶ Combine sounds to form words and check with the letters.

▶ Match sounds to letters in words.

▶ Divide words into separate sounds and match to letters.

Children love poetry with rhythm and rhyme; the language of poetry sings inside their heads. As they grow in experience, they also learn to appreciate poetry that does not rhyme and the sensory images and unique perspectives it evokes. Poetry is related to the many cultures from which children come; by sharing cultures, they construct the common experiences of childhood.

In addition, poetry provides resources for the heart and spirit. Immersing children in simple poetry at an early age helps to instill a lifelong habit of enjoying language and seeking out poetry in order to expand one's vision. Poetry joins us to the past and to our fellow human beings in the present.

VALUES AND GOALS OF POETRY IN THE SECOND GRADE CLASSROOM

Poetry expands children's oral language abilities as it:

- Builds a repertoire of the unique patterns and forms of language.
- Helps children become sensitive to and enjoy the sounds of language—rhymes, alliteration, assonance, onomatopoeia *(buzz, whiz, woof)*.
- Supports articulation and elocution.
- Extends listening and speaking vocabularies.
- Expands knowledge of the complex syntax of language.
- Encourages children to manipulate and play with language.
- Develops phonological awareness (rhyme, syllables, onsets and rimes).
- Develops phonemic awareness (the ability to manipulate individual sounds).
- Makes it easy for children to isolate and identify sounds, take words apart, and change sounds in words to make new words.
- Provides rich examples of comparisons such as similes and metaphors.

Poetry expands children's written language abilities as it:

- Expands spoken vocabulary, making it easier later for them to read words.
- Provides the opportunity to share in the reading of familiar materials, behaving as readers by following print from left to right and matching word by word.
- Provides a supported situation within which the can learn high frequency words.
- Provides opportunities to connect words by the way they look or sound.
- Helps them notice the letters and letter patterns associated with sounds.
- Helps them notice letters that are embedded in words and that words that are embedded in extended text.
- Provides examples of different kinds of words—compound words, base words, contractions, plurals, words with inflectional endings (like *ing, ed*), homophones, homographs, synonyms, and antonyms.
- Provides the opportunity to participate in fluent, phrased reading.

Poetry expands children's content knowledge as it:

- Provides new perceptions and ideas for them to think about.
- Encourages them to develop a sense of humor.
- Sensitizes them to the forms and style of poetry.

Poetry contributes to children's social knowledge and skills as it:

- Provides artistic and aesthetic experiences.
- Creates a sense of community through enjoying rhymes and songs as a group.
- Gives them access to English-speaking culture.
- Provides a window to many other cultures.
- Creates memories of shared enjoyable times.

The Elements of Poetry

The following elements provide the essence of poetry's appeal. In the poems appropriate for young children, language patterns, rhyme, rhythm, and humor dominate, but all the elements are present.

RHYME

While not all poems rhyme, many of the simple poems children enjoy include words that have alliterative beginning parts (*onsets*) and/or assonant ending parts (*rimes*). The onset of a syllable is the consonant or consonant cluster that starts the word. The rime is the vowel and everything after the first part. So the onset of *duck* is *d* and the onset of *stuck* is *st*. The rime of *duck* is *uck,* and *uck* is also the rime of *stuck.* Words that have the same rime also rhyme. Rhyme is appealing and memorable; rhyme always refers to the sound of the ending part of the word, not necessarily the spelling. Many of us can recall simple rhymes that we learned as children. Notice the rhyme in "Walk Fast," even though the words *snow, slow, go,* and *toe* are not spelled the same:

> Walk fast in snow,
> In frost walk slow,
> And still as you go,
> Tread on your toe.
> When frost and snow are both together
> Sit by the fire and spare shoe leather.

RHYTHM

Poetry involves both simple and complex rhythms. There is often a "beat" to the language, which, again, makes it memorable and enjoyable, especially when chanted in unison. Take "Stepping Stones," for example:

> Stepping over stepping stones, one, two, three,
> Stepping over stepping stones, come with me.
> The river's very fast,
> And the river's very wide,
> And we'll step across on stepping stones
> And reach the other side.

FIGURATIVE LANGUAGE

Poetry often evokes sensory images by making comparisons (similes and metaphors), as in "Jack Frost":

Jack Frost bites your noses.

He chills your cheeks and freezes your toes.

He comes every year when winter is here

And stays until spring is near.

Another example is from Sara Coleridge's "The Months of the Year":

March brings breezes loud and shrill,

Stirs the dancing daffodil.

Often rhymes, chants, and songs contain onomatopoetic language (words like *whoosh* that sound like the phenomenon they represent). Take this example from "The Thunderstorm":

Boom, bang, boom, bang

Rumpety, lumpety, bump!

Zoom, zam, zoom, zam,

Clippity, clappity, clump!

Rustles and bustles

And swishes and zings!

What wonderful sounds

A thunderstorm brings.

LANGUAGE PATTERNS

Rhymes and poems are most enjoyable because of the language patterns that are included. *Alliteration*, the repetition of consonant sounds, is evident in "The Tutor":

A tutor who tooted the flute

Tried to tutor two tooters to toot.

Said the two to the tutor,

"Is it harder to toot, or

To tutor two tooters to toot?"

Children love these tongue twisters, and they are an excellent way to help them internalize initial sounds. Here is another good example:

Robert Rowley rolled a round roll 'round;

A round roll Robert Rowley rolled 'round.

If Robert Rowley rolled a round roll 'round,

Where rolled the round roll Robert Rowley rolled 'round?

Assonance, the repetition of vowel sounds, is evident in "Moses Supposes":

Moses supposes his toeses are roses,

But Moses supposes erroneously;

For nobody's toeses are posies of roses,

As Moses supposes his toeses to be.

REPETITION

Many poems, particularly songs, have repeating stanzas or phrases, such as "Mary Wore a Red Dress." Another example is "Autumn Leaves":

Autumn leaves are falling, falling, falling

Autumn leaves are spinning, spinning, spinning

Autumn leaves are floating, floating, floating.

Autumn leaves are turning, turning, turning.

Autumn leaves are dancing, dancing, dancing.

Autumn leaves are blowing, blowing, blowing.

Autumn leaves are falling, falling, falling.

Autumn leaves are sleeping, sleeping, sleeping.

Rhythmic repetition like this helps children learn these rhymes easily; many have been set to music and can be sung, such as "The Mulberry Bush."

SENSORY IMAGES

Poetry can induce laughter or tears with just a few words because this condensed form of language plays on the senses. Poets evoke memories, form visual images, point up absurdities, and help us enter unique worlds. Christina Rosetti's "Who Has Seen the Wind?" gives us a visual image of the wind:

Who has seen the wind?

Neither you nor I.

But when the trees bow down their heads

The wind is passing by.

Selecting Poetry for Young Children

When using poetry with young children it is helpful to think in terms of the complexity of language and concepts. Also, will the children experience the poems orally or do you expect them to process the print? Children can listen to and recite more complex poems than they can read. Carefully consider the characteristics of the texts you use for shared reading to be sure they are within the range of children's independent reading after many opportunities for shared reading. The first poems children encounter should be very simple in terms of:

▶ Length and number of words.

▶ Decodability.

▶ Ratio of easy to harder high frequency words.

▶ Sentence or phrase structure.

▶ Vocabulary (although children may enjoy many rhymes without knowing the precise meaning of some archaic words, such as "pease porridge").

▶ Ideas; for example, visual imagery and metaphor require more of the child than simple rhymes and songs.

The poems in this book represent a gradient of difficulty. At the beginning of the year, select very simple poems, gradually increasing the level of challenge. The poems in the chart below illustrate a continuum of difficulty.

① SIMPLEST	② MORE DIFFICULT	③ MOST DIFFICULT
Apples, Peaches	**Sing Your Way Home**	**December Leaves**
Apples, peaches,	Sing your way home	The fallen leaves are cornflakes
Pears, plums,	At the close of the day.	That fill the lawn's wide dish,
Tell me when your	Sing your way home	And night and noon
Birthday comes.	Drive the shadows away.	The wind's a spoon
	Smile every mile,	That stirs them with a swish.
	For wherever you roam	The sky's a silver sifter
	It will brighten your road,	A-sifting white and slow,
	It will lighten your load,	That gently shakes
	If you sing your way home.	On crisp brown flakes
		The sugar known as snow.

Verse 1 is both simple and short. The theme is easy; there are few syllables; there is repetition. Children can say it over and over, in a circle game. Verse 2 has longer lines and more complex ideas, but the imagery is easy to grasp and the rhythm helps children learn it. Verse 3, "December Leaves," is about the same length as "Sing Your Way Home," but the metaphors are more complex. The imagery demands more of the reader. Of the three selections, only number three could truly be called a poem by literary definition.

As you select poems to share, consider your children's previous experience, skill with language, and vocabulary. If you begin with easy poems and they learn them very quickly (for example, they join in during shared reading and remember them), you can provide slightly more complex examples.

Planning for Teaching Opportunities When Revisiting a Text

As short texts, poems provide a multitude of opportunities for learning about language. After enjoying a poem several times, you may want to revisit the text with children to help them notice letter patterns and make connections between words. The following grid helps you think about the varied opportunities in particular texts. In each box we list possible elements to show, reinforce, or help children notice within a poem. You can try planning some poems out for yourself in advance (see the blank form following the filled-in chart) or use the blank grid to keep a record of your teaching points within each poem as you make them.

WORD ANALYSIS TEACHING OPPORTUNITIES WHEN REVISITING POETRY

Title	Type of Text (e.g., limerick, tongue twister; couplet, free verse)	Phonogram Patterns (e.g., -at, -ig, -oan, -ait, -ate)	Letter-Sound (beginning or ending consonants and clusters)	High Frequency Words	Other (e.g., syllables, contractions, suffixes/inflectional endings, compound words, plurals, ending consonants/clusters/ digraphs, concept words like colors and numbers, names)
One, Two, Buckle My Shoe	nursery rhyme 5 rhyming pairs	-ick, -ay, -em, -aight, -ig, -at, -en	b, m, d, p, f, h, sh, th, st, str	my, the, up, them, at	numerals number words
Apples, Peaches	4-line poem with alternate line rhyme	-ell, -en, -um, -ear, -each	p, t, m, c, y, b	me, when, your, come	concept of fruit compound word (birthday) plurals with s, es
Bat, Bat	5-line verse with 2 rhyming pairs of lines	-at, -and, -ice, -en, -ake	b, c, m, h, g, y, b, g, n, wh	come, my, and, you, when, if, am, not	Contraction (I'll) multisyllable words (bacon, mistaken)
Betty Botter	rhythmic, alliterative poem a tongue twister	-utter, -itter, -atter, -it, -ill, -ake	b, s, p	bought, but, put, some, she said, this, in my, it, will, make	assonance (repetition of vowel sounds) words with er ending
At the Seaside	2 verses with 3 sets of rhyming words	-ea, -own, -ade, -ave, -ore, -ole, -ame, -up, -ill, -old	w, d, s, g, m, h, c, t, n	when, I, was, they, like, were, up	compound word (seaside) rhyming words multisyllable words (wooden, beside, hollow)

WORD ANALYSIS TEACHING OPPORTUNITIES WHEN REVISITING POETRY

Title	Type of Text (e.g., limerick, tongue twister, couplet, free verse)	Phonogram Patterns (e.g., -at, -ig, -oan, -ait, -ate)	Letter-Sound (beginning or ending consonants and clusters)	High Frequency Words	Other (e.g., syllables, contractions, suffixes/inflectional endings, compound words, plurals, ending consonants/clusters/ digraphs, concept words like colors and numbers, names)

Tools for Using Poetry

The tools for working with poetry are simple. You will want to have them well organized and readily available for quick lessons. We suggest the following:

▶ **EASEL**

a vertical surface for displaying chart paper or the pocket chart that is large enough for all children to see and sturdy enough to avoid tipping.

▶ **POCKET CHART**

a stiff piece of cardboard or plastic that has lines with grooves into which cards can be inserted so that children can work with lines of poems and/or individual words.

▶ **MASKS**

cutout cardboard shapes designed to outline words on charts for children to use in locating words or parts of words (see templates in "Materials and Routines," *Phonics Lessons, 2, Teaching Resources*).

▶ **HIGHLIGHTER TAPE**

transparent stick-on tape that can be used to emphasize words, letters, or word parts.

▶ **STICK-ON NOTES**

small pieces of paper that have a sticky backing and can temporarily be used to conceal words or parts of words so that children can attend to them.

▶ **FLAGS**

a handle with a flat piece of wood or cardboard on the end that can be placed under a word on a chart as a way to locate or emphasize it (see templates in "Materials and Routines," *Phonics Lessons, 2, Teaching Resources*)

▶ **TAGS**

signs with concise directions so that children can remember an independent work activity; for example: *Read, Mix, Fix, Read* (*Read* the poem, *Mix* up the sentence strips of a poem, *Fix* the poem back together, and *Read* it again to check it).

▶ **ART MATERIALS**

media such as paint, glue, colored paper, tissue paper.

Instructional Contexts for Poetry

There are several instructional contexts within which you can use rhymes and poems effectively. For more information on instructional practices see Fountas and Pinnell (1996) *Guided Reading: Good First Teaching For All Children* and Pinnell and Fountas (1998) *Word Matters: Teaching Phonics and Spelling in the Reading/Writing Classroom.* Poetry fits well into the range of activities typical in second grade classrooms.

INTERACTIVE READ-ALOUD

Reading aloud forms a foundation for language and literacy development, and poetry is meant to be read orally. In addition, reading aloud provides a model of fluent phrased reading. There are many wonderful picture books that present rhyming verse to children in a very engaging way. *The Itsy Bitsy Spider* (Trapani 1993) is an illustrated variation of the familiar verse. *Pignic* (Miranda 1996) is a wonderful rhyming (and repetitive consonant sounds) alphabet book in which a family of twenty-six pigs have a picnic with all kinds of food. *Chicka Chicka Boom Boom* (Martin and Archambault 1989) is another rhyming alphabet book with wonderful rhythm and a focus on uppercase and lowercase letters. You can also read individual poems from volumes such as *Tomie dePaola's Mother Goose* (1985) or Kay Chorao's *Knock at the Door* (1999), a book of action rhymes.

We recommend repeated readings of favorite poems or rhyming books; it takes many repetitions for children to be able to join in. Ask them to listen the first two or three times you read a verse, but encourage them to join in after they have grasped enough to say it with you, especially on a refrain. In this way, children will begin to internalize much of the language and enjoy it more.

SHARED READING

Shared reading involves children's both hearing the verse and seeing the print. As they join in, they will get the feel of fluent, expressive reading. You use an enlarged text—a chart that you have prepared or purchased or a big book. Using this shared approach allows you to demonstrate pointing while reading. After one or two repetitions, encourage children to read with you in an interactive read-aloud. Be sure that all children can see the visual display of print. You'll want to sit or stand to the side and use a thin pointer (pointers that have objects like "hands" on the end usually block children's view of the very word you are pointing out). The idea is to maximize children's attention to the print. Shared reading helps them learn how the eyes work in reading. They'll also learn more about rhyme and rhythm.

CHORAL READING AND PERFORMANCE

Choral reading is a more sophisticated version of shared reading. Participants may read from an enlarged text, but often they have their own individual copies. They may have a leader, but it is not always necessary for the leader to point to the words. Participants can practice reading together several times and then perform the piece. There can be assigned "solo" lines, boys' and girls' lines, question and response lines, or the whole group can read all the lines. Emphasize varying the voice to suit the meaning of the poem. You can add sound effects (wooden sticks, bells, or other simple tools) or simply have children clap or snap their fingers to accentuate words or phrases.

RECITATION

It is very useful for children to commit some poems to memory. Chances are, these poems will stay with them in some form throughout their lives. Choosing a favorite poem and saying it enough times to remember it helps children learn to sustain attention and, again, to internalize rich language. Often, poems expand vocabulary. When poems are memorized, they can be recited for the class or others. This activity shouldn't cause anxiety; you can incorporate it into the classroom matter-of-factly. Let the student choose: this ensures the appropriate level of difficulty, and the task will be more enjoyable.

INDEPENDENT READING

Children love reading poetry, searching for favorite poems, and illustrating poems. A personal poetry book or anthology becomes a treasure. After poems have been read in shared reading, you can reproduce them on smaller pieces of paper. Children glue the poems in a composition book or spiral notebook and illustrate them. Be sure that you are using poems that they are familiar with and can read. Reading their personal poetry books is a good independent reading activity. You can increase the complexity of poems for second graders.

WRITING POETRY

Children can begin to get a feel for writing verse through interactive writing (see McCarrier, Pinnell and Fountas (2000) *Interactive Writing: How Language and Literacy Come Together K–2*). In interactive writing, you and the children compose a message together. You act as a scribe, using the easel, but occasionally children come up and write in a word or letter when you want to draw attention to it.

You can substitute their names in a verse or create a variation of one of their favorites (for example, for "Brown Bear, Brown Bear, What do you see?" substitute "Black Cat, Black Cat, What do you see?"). This activity gives them power over language, and they may want to experiment on their own.

You can also help children see how to create a poem and to realize that a poem does not have to rhyme. In writer's workshop, children may describe an event or scene that lends itself to poetry. You can help them reshape the written piece by taking out unnecessary words and laying it out as a poem. As children hear many examples of poems, they will want to write their own.

Maintaining individual poetry anthologies often prompts children to try writing their own poems on themes and in forms similar to their choices. Encouraging this experimentation helps them use language in new ways.

Types of Poetry

Poetry can be categorized in many different ways—by pattern, structure, or topic, for example. This book includes rhymes and poems in many different categories, related to both forms and themes. Many of the poems can be placed in more than one category.

NURSERY RHYMES

Traditional rhymes by anonymous poets have been passed down over generations. There are often many different versions. Originally serving as political satire for adults, they have been loved by children for generations. They usually rhyme in couplets or alternating lines and are highly rhythmic. Young children enjoy these simple verses, and they help to build a foundation that will later lead them to a more sophisticated appreciation of poetry. The "Mother Goose" rhymes, which were published in the eighteenth century, are the best known, but equivalents exist around the world. An example children love is "Humpty Dumpty":

Humpty Dumpty sat on a wall.

Humpty Dumpty had a great fall;

And all the king's horses and all the king's men

Couldn't put Humpty together again.

RHYMED VERSE

Many poems for young children have lines that end with words that rhyme. These may be rhyming couplets (each pair of lines rhyme), as in "Five Fat Turkeys":

Five fat turkeys are we.

We slept all night in a tree.

When the cook came around,

We couldn't be found.

So, that's why we're here, you see.

Or, every other line may rhyme, as in "The Swing," by Robert Louis Stevenson:

How do you like to go up in a swing,

Up in the air so blue?

Oh, I do think it the pleasantest thing

Ever a child can do!

There are a variety of other rhyming patterns. You may even see verses where every line rhymes, as in "I Scream" or almost rhymes as in "Denise Sees the Fleece":

Denise sees the fleece

Denise sees the fleas.

At least Denise could sneeze

And feed and freeze the fleas.

FREE VERSE (UNRHYMED)

Many poems evoke sensory images and sometimes have rhythm, but do not rhyme. Haiku poems, for example, have a defined number of syllables; these "spare" poems evoke visual images. An example is "Snow" by Issa:

I could eat it!

This snow that falls

So softly, so softly.

Here's an example of an action verse that has rhythm but does not rhyme—"Knock at the Door":

Knock at the door. [*Knocking motion*]

Lift the latch. [*Lifting motion*]

And walk right in. [*Actual or "finger" walking, then pantomiming hello*]

WORD PLAY

Some poems play with words by juxtaposing interesting word patterns in a humorous and playful way, like "Eletelephony," by Laura E. Richards:

Once there was an elephant,

Who tried to use the telephant—

No! No! I mean an elephone

Who tried to use the telephone—

(Dear Me! I am not certain quite

That even now I've got it right.)

How'e'er it was, he got his trunk

Entangled in the telephunk;

The more he tried to get it free,

The louder buzzed the telephee—

(I fear I'd better drop the song

Of elephop and telephong!)

In word play we also include tongue twisters (poems that play with words in a way that makes them very difficult to recite without stumbling because the words are difficult to pronounce one after another). A well-known example is "She Sells Seashells":

> She sells sea shells
>
> On the seashore.
>
> The shells that she sells
>
> Are seashells I'm sure.
>
> So if she sells seashells
>
> On the seashore
>
> I'm sure that the shells
>
> Are seashore shells.

HUMOROUS VERSE

Humorous verse draws children's attention to absurdities as well as to the sounds and rhythms of language. Sometimes these humorous verses tell stories—for example, "There Was an Old Person of Ware":

> There was an old person of Ware,
>
> Who rode on the back of a bear.
>
> When they asked, "Does it trot?"
>
> He said, "Certainly not!
>
> He's a Moppsikon Floppsikon bear!"

Edward Lear's verse is a limerick, a highly structured form in which the first two lines rhyme, the second two lines rhyme, and the fifth line rhymes with the first two.

SONGS

Songs are musical texts originally intended to be sung. An example is "Do Your Ears Hang Low?":

_____

Do your ears hang low?

Do they wobble to and fro?

Can you tie them in a knot?

Can you tie them in a bow?

Can you throw them o'er your shoulder,

Like a Continental Soldier

Do your ears hang low?

You may know the traditional tunes to the songs we have included in this volume, but if you don't, you can compose your own tune or simply have children chant them, enjoying the rhythm and rhyme.

ACTION SONGS AND POEMS

Action poems involve action along with rhythm and rhyme. An example is "Itsy Bitsy Spider":

_____

The itsy, bitsy spider [*Two hands, fingers together—touch finger to thumb on other hand.*]

Climbed up the waterspout. [*Make crawling motions up.*]

Down came the rain [*Flutter fingers down.*]

And washed the spider out. [*Open hands.*]

Out came the sun [*Arms form round ball.*]

And dried up all the rain. [*Hands flutter up.*]

And the itsy, bitsy spider [*Repeat crawling motions.*]

Climbed up the spout again.

This category also includes jump-rope songs, traditional rhymes that children originally chanted while they jumped rope. An example is "Miss Mary Mack":

Miss Mary Mack, Mack, Mack

All dressed in black, black, black

With silver buttons, buttons, buttons

All down her back, back, back.

Children can chant and act out jump-rope songs.

There are also chants that accompany games or are simply enjoyable to say together. Chants are like songs in that they have rhythm and rhyme, but they are meant to be spoken in chorus rather than set to music. They can also be nonsense rhymes—for example, "A Sailor Went to Sea":

A sailor went to sea, sea, sea,

To see what he could see, see, see.

But all that he could see, see, see,

Was the bottom of the deep blue sea, sea, sea.

CONCEPT POEMS

Poems in this category focus on concepts such as numbers, days of the week, colors, ordinal words, seasons, and any other category of information. An example is "Bunnies' Bedtime":

"My bunnies must go to bed,"

The little mother rabbit said.

"But I will count them first to see

If they have all come back to me.

One bunny, two bunnies, three bunnies dear.

Four bunnies, five bunnies—yes, all are here.

They are the prettiest things alive—

My bunnies, one, two, three, four, five."

These verses are not only engaging but also easy to learn. As children learn them, they will be repeating the vocabulary that surrounds important concepts. "Four Seasons" presents words that evoke sensory images related to seasons:

Spring is showery, flowery, bowery.

Summer, hoppy, croppy, poppy.

Autumn, slippy, drippy, nippy.

Winter, breezy, sneezy, freezy.

In the category of concept poems, we also include name poems, which really transcend categories. Many verses present a wonderful opportunity to substitute children's names for names or words already there. An example is "Bullfrog":

Here's Mr. Bullfrog,

Sitting on a rock.

Along comes _____.

Mr. Bullfrog jumps, KERPLOP!

Many of the verses in other sections of the book also offer opportunities for similar innovations, so look for opportunities. Children will love substituting their own words and phrases. They will develop ownership for the writing and become more sensitive to rhymes, syllables, and word patterns in the process.

Fifty Ways to Use Poems–Plus!

Below we suggest fifty specific ways to use the poems in this volume. Plus, you will notice that each poem includes an instructional suggestion— an easy way to refine and extend the learning and enjoyment potential of each poem. You will find many more ways to engage your children in joyful play with oral and written language. The rich collection of poems in this volume can be reproduced, analyzed, or simply read aloud. Enjoy!

1.	**MARCHING TO RHYMES**	Marching around the room while chanting a poem will help children feel the rhythm.
2.	**FLANNELBOARDS**	Make flannelboard figures for favorite nursery rhyme characters. Children can say the rhyme as they move figures around. You can also glue felt or attach Velcro to the back of pictures that students have drawn on card stock.
3.	**STORYBOARDS**	Have students draw or paint a backdrop that represents the scene from a rhyme or song. Then have them make cutout figures and glue them on popsicle sticks so that they can move the puppets around in front of the backdrop.
4.	**LISTENING FOR RHYMES**	Have children clap or snap their fingers when they come to a rhyming word. They can also say the rhyming word softer (or louder) or mouth the word without making a sound.
5.	**RESPONDING**	Divide the class in half. Taking a familiar poem, have half the group read (or say) the poem up to the rhyming word and then stop. Let the other half of the class shout the rhyming word.
6.	**POEMS ON TAPE**	Record specific poems on a tape so that children can listen independently at a listening center. Include card stock copies of the poems, and show children how to follow along with the recording.
7.	**CLASS POETRY TAPE**	As children learn poems, gradually add to a class tape of their poetry reading or chanting. Keep a table of contents for the tape on a chart and/or place the taped poems in a book. Children can listen to the tape while following along in the book.

8. POEM PICTURES	After reading a poem aloud at different times of the day, have children make pictures to go with it and display them with the poem. Duplicate individual copies of a simple poem and ask each child to illustrate it.
9. WORD ENDINGS	Write the poem in large print on a chart or on strips for a pocket chart. After many readings of a poem on a large chart, help children notice words that rhyme and specific vocabulary. They can use a masking card or highlighter tape to mark these words, for extra illustration space, photocopy the poem on 8 1/2 x 14, or larger, paper.
10. POEM INNOVATIONS	Engage children in noticing and using the language syntax in the poem to create their own similar versions. For example, insert different names in "Jack Be Nimble" or different foods in "I Like Chocolate."
11. PERSONAL POETRY BOOKS	Have children make their own personal poetry books by gluing the poems they have experienced in shared reading into spiral notebooks and then illustrating them. Over time they will have a large personal collection of poems to take home.
12. LITTLE POEM BOOKS	Make individual poem books, with one line of a poem on each page (for example, "One, Two, Buckle My Shoe"); children can illustrate each page, read the book, and take it home.
13. POEM PERFORMANCES	Children can perform the poems after they learn them, sometimes adding sound effects with rhythm instruments such as sticks and drums or by clapping and snapping their fingers.
14. RESPONSIVE READING	Find poems such as "Are You Sleeping?" that lend themselves to recitation by two or more speakers. Groups of children read questions and answers or alternate lines.
15. POETRY PLAY	Lead children in saying their favorite poems while they line up, as they walk through an area in which their talking will not disturb other classes, or any time they have a moment or two of "wait time."
16. LINE-UP POEMS	When passing out of the room for recess or lunch, play games in which children say or finish a line of a poem in order to take their place in line.

17. RHYMING CLOZE	Read poems, asking children to join in only on the rhyming words. Put highlighter tape on the rhyming words.
18. FINGER POEMS AND ACTION POEMS	Make finger plays from poems. Do poems with motions involving the entire body. We have included finger-play and action directions for many poems, but you can make up many more.
19. POEM POSTERS	Use art materials (colored and/or textured paper, pens, crayons, paints) to illustrate poems on charts for the whole group to enjoy, or individually in personal poetry books.
20. POEMS WITH BLANKS	Give children individual copies of poems with a blank space in which they can write their names.
21. MYSTERY WORDS	In shared reading of a familiar poem, leave out key words but put in the first letter so that children can check their reading.
22. POEM DISPLAYS	Display a poem in several places in the room; children find the poem and use chopstick pointers to read it in small and large versions in different places.
23. POETRY BOX	Make a poetry box that contains slightly enlarged and illustrated versions of familiar poems; children can take them out and read them to a buddy.
24. POETRY BOARD	Make a theme poetry board using poems that explore a concept (for example, animals or vegetables).
25. TONGUE TWISTERS	Make up tongue twisters using the names of children in the class and have them illustrate the verses; for example Carol carries cookies, carrots, candy, and cucumbers in a cart.
26. POCKET CHART	Place poems on sentence strips in a pocket chart for a variety of activities: • Substituting words to innovate on the text; • Highlighting words, letters, or parts of words with colored transparent plastic or highlighter tape; • Putting sentence strips in order and reading; • Masking words; • Placing cards over words to predict and then check predictions with the print.
27. POEM PUZZLES	Have the children cut a poem into strips, mix them up, order them, and glue them on paper in the correct order. Then have them use art materials to illustrate the text. You can create a simple strip template to photocopy for many different poems.

28. CONCEPT POEMS	Place poems on particular topics at appropriate places in the classroom. For example, place a poem about windows on the window, one about trees on a window that looks out at a tree, or one about flowers next to a vase of flowers.
29. SEQUENCING POEMS	Second graders could have separate pages that they first put in order, staple together as a book, illustrate the pages, and then read the book to others.
30. MORE SONGS AND POEMS	Be on the alert for popular songs that children like or street rhymes that they know. Take appropriate verses from these songs and add them to the poetry collection.
31. POEM PLAYS	Create a "play" from the poem. Read the poem (children may join in) while several children act it out.
32. POETRY DRESS-UP	Collect some simple "dress up" items related to the rhymes and poems in your collection. Invite the children to dress up for the poem reading.
33. POETRY PARTY	Have a party to which everyone comes dressed as a character from a poem. (Props may be made of paper.) The group has to guess which poem is represented and then read the poem to the child representing that character.
34. CHARACTER BULLETIN BOARD	Each child draws a favorite character from a poem and then cuts the figure out. Use interactive writing to create labels for each character on the board.
35. PUPPET SHOW	Have the children make and use finger, stick, or hand puppets to say the poem.
36. POETRY AND PROSE	Take a poem and create a "prose" version of it. Place the two versions of the story beside each other so that children can see and talk about differences in language, form, punctuation, mood, etc.
37. POETRY PICNIC	Many poems have something to do with food. For example, "curds and whey" is cottage cheese. After children have learned a lot of verses, make a list of foods. Children can bring some of them or you can bring them. Then, they say the poem and eat the food.
38. POETRY PAIRS	Children find two poems that go together in some way. They bring the two poems to sharing time and tell how they are alike. You can make a class book of poem pairs with (illustrated) connected poems on opposite pages.

39. POETRY LANDSCAPE MURAL	Children paint a background on which they can glue different poetry characters. This mural requires some planning. For example, you would want a hill with flowers, a sky, and a small city below for "Afternoon on a Hill."
40. POETRY SORT	Have a box of poems on cards that children know very well and can read. They can read the poems and sort them in any way they want to—theme (happy, silly, sad), topic (mice, girls, boys, bears), the way they rhyme (two lines, every other line, no rhyme).
41. POEMS IN SHAPES	Have children read a poem and then glue it on a shape (give them a template) that represents it. For example, a zig zag shape for "The Zig Zag Boy and Girl."
42. MIXED-UP POEM	Place a familiar poem on sentence strips in the pocket chart. Mix it up and have children help you rebuild it by saying the lines and looking for the next one. You can also have a correct model displayed beside the cutup version so that they can check it. Soon children will be able to perform this action on their own.
43. PICTURE WORDS	Have children draw pictures for key words in a poem and display them right above the word on a chart.
44. HUNTING FOR WORDS	Using flyswatters with rectangular holes in the center (or masking cards), have children hunt for particular words or words that rhyme with or start like another.
45. WORD LOCATION	Have a familiar poem in the pocket chart but with some blanks. Give children some key words. Stop when you come to the key word and ask who has it. Children will need to think about beginning sounds and letters.
46. WORD MATCH	Place one line of a poem in the pocket chart and have children rebuild the line by matching individual words under the line.
47. LINE POEM	Give a group of children one word each of a poem, written in large print on a card. The rest of the class lines up these children so that the word order is correct. Then they take turns walking down the line and saying the poem by pointing to each child and his or her word.

48. LOCATING HIGH FREQUENCY WORDS

The words children encounter over and over in poems will form a core of words that they know and can recognize rapidly. You can have children locate the words to draw attention to them. They can also match word cards by placing like words on top of the words in the poem. An interesting exercise is to create high frequency words in different fonts. Be sure the words are clear and recognizable. Matching these words to words on a chart or in the pocket chart creates an additional challenge in looking at the features of letters.

49. POETRY NEWSLETTER

Send home a monthly newsletter that tells parents the poems children have learned and provides some poems they can sing or say at home.

50. CLASS POETRY BOOK

Collect favorite poems into a class book that is small enough to be portable. Children take turns taking the book home. They can read the poems to stuffed animal or family members.

Poetry Links to Phonics Lessons

In *Phonics Lessons: Letters, Words, and How They Work, Grade 2,* you will find under LINK, Shared Reading recommendations that enable you to connect learning across the Language and Literacy Framework. Often, the shared reading recommendations suggest you turn to *Sing A Song of Poetry* for instructional follow-up using particular poems, songs, and verse. This list links many phonics lessons to a specific poem that extends and refines the instructional aim of the lesson; however, you will notice that not all lessons are linked to a poem and, sometimes, a lesson is linked to two or more poems. What does this mean? The links are completely flexible! Feel free to find and make your own links, and do not feel compelled to use every poem we recommend.

The primary goal of this collection is, quite literally, to "sing a song of poetry"! Invite your children to chant, recite, echo, and play with the poems. Above all, *Sing A Song of Poetry* is meant to inspire a love of language.

Letter/Sound Relationships

LS 1	The Bear; The Goat; The Months of the Year
LS 2	Away Down East; Miss Mary Mack
LS 3	A Caterpillar Crawled; I Live in the City
LS 4	Jack Sprat; Over the River; Two Times Table
LS 5	December Leaves; Good Morning, Merry Sunshine; The Months of the Year
LS 6	A Lady Went A-marketing; The Littlest Worm
LS 7	The Caterpillar; The Chickens; Mary Wore Her Red Dress
LS 8	Caterpillar; Fuzzy Little Caterpillar; The Secret
LS 9	Buffalo Gals; Mr. Nobody
LS 10	There Was an Old Man With a Beard; A Thunderstorm
LS 11	Donkey, Donkey; Fuzzy Little Caterpillar; Jelly on the Plate; Little Arabella Miller; What is Pink?
LS 12	The Greedy Man; Jelly on the Plate

LS 13	The Chickens; The Months of the Year
LS 14	The Centipede's Song; The City Mouse and the Garden Mouse
LS 15	The Donut Song; The Land of Counterpane
LS 16	The Months of the Year; Where Go the Boats?
LS 17	The Bear; Row, Row, Row Your Boat; Slowly, Slowly; Sneeze on Monday
LS 18	The Boy Stood in the Supper Room; Star Light, Star Bright; Stepping Stones
LS 19	My Shadow; Two Little Feet
LS 20	Fuzzy Little Caterpillar; The Months of the Year
LS 21	Bow-Wow, Says the Dog
LS 22	Aiken Drum, As I Was Going to Banbury; The Hobbyhorse
LS 23	One, Two, Buckle My Shoe; Rock-a-bye Baby

Spelling Patterns

SP 1	Snowman; When I Was One
SP 2	Miss Mary Mack; Spread It Thick
SP 3	Birds of a Feather; A Mouse in Her Room
SP 4	Bat, Bat; Calico Pie
SP 5	Queen, Queen Caroline (-*ine*); Stepping Stones (-*ide*); There Was an Old Man from Dumbree (-*ice*)
SP 6	
SP 7	If All the World Were Apple Pie (-*ink*); The North Wond Doth Blow (-ing); Once I Saw a Bunny (-*ink*); The Swing (-*ing*)
SP 8	My Father Is Extremely Tall; The Postman

SP 9	Buffalo Gals; The Cupboard; Denise Sees the Fleece
SP 10	Fuzzy Little Caterpillar; Mr. Noobody; Silly Simon
SP 11	The Goat (-*ain*); Slowly, Slowly (-*ail*); The Squirrel (-*ail*)
SP 12	Jack-in-the-box; Star Light, Star Bright
SP 13	Row, Row, Row Your Boat
SP 14	Owl; Pairs or Pears
SP 15	Bat, Bat; They That Wash on Monday
SP 16	The Chickens; December Leaves
SP 17	If All the World Were Apple Pie (*ee*); Old Mother Hubbard (*oa*); Over in the Meadow (*ea*)

High Frequency Words

HF 1	As I Was Going Along; Dig a Little Hole; Great A; One, Two, Three, Four, Five; To Market, To Market
HF 2	Cock-Crow; Fiddle-de-de; I'm a Little Teapot; Jack-in-the-Box; This Old Man
HF 3	Baby Mice; Billy, Billy; I Have a Little Wagon; The Swing
HF 4	Down at the Station; Milkman, Milkman; Old Mother Hubbard; Pease Porridge; Where Are You?

HF 5	Billy, Billy; Jack Sprat; Little Bird; There Was an Old Woman; Wheels on the Bus
HF 6	Are You Sleeping; The Cat and the Fiddle; The Grand Old Duke of York; Here We Go Around the Mulberry Bush; The Swing
HF 7	I Clap My Hands; Jelly on the Plate; Little Red Apple

Word Meaning

Word Structure

Word Solving Actions

A, My Name Is Alice

A, my name is Alice,
And my husband's name is Al.
We come from Alabama,
And we sell apples.

B, my name is Barbara,
And my husband's name is Bob.
We come from Boston,
And we sell beans.

C, my name is Carol,
And my husband's name is Carl.
We come from Chicago,
And we sell carts.

D, my name is Donna,
And my husband's name is Dave.
We come from Denver,
And we sell doughnuts.

E, my name is Ellen,
And my husband's name is Ed.
We come from Evanston,
And we sell eggs.

F, my name is Frances,
And my husband's name is Frank.
We come from Florida,
And we sell frankfurters.

SUGGESTION: Children will enjoy creating verses for the rest of the letters of the alphabet. After the class has had several oral experiences with this alphabet-game poem, invite them to create an illustrated class book highlighting their own first names. Each child can illustrate one page with felt pen drawings or cut-paper art.

Afternoon on a Hill

by Edna St. Vincent Millay

I will be the gladdest thing

Under the sun.

I will touch a hundred flowers

And not pick one.

I will look at cliffs and clouds

With quiet eyes,

Watch the wind bow down the grass,

And the grass rise.

And when lights begin to show

Up from the town,

I will mark which must be mine,

And then start down!

SUGGESTION: Millay's poem is a beautiful one to recite together, making motions to indicate gladness, the sun, flowers on the hill, etc. The poem could stimulate a discussion about caring for the earth and valuing living and growing things. Pair with the picture book *Miss Rumphius*, by Barbara Cooney.

Aiken Drum

There was a man lived in the moon,
Lived in the moon, lived in the moon.
There was a man lived in the moon,
And his name was Aiken Drum.

Refrain

    And he played upon a ladle,

    A ladle, a ladle,

    He played upon a ladle,

    And his name was Aiken Drum.

And his hat was made of good cream cheese,
Of good cream cheese, of good cream cheese,
And his hat was made of good cream cheese,
And his name was Aiken Drum.

Refrain

ADDITIONAL VERSES:
And his coat was made of good roast beef,
Of good roast beef, of good roast beef,
And his coat was made of good roast beef,
And his name was Aiken Drum.

Refrain

And his pants were made of plastic bags,
Of plastic bags, of plastic bags,
And his pants were made of plastic bags,
And his name was Aiken Drum.

Refrain

SUGGESTION: This rhyme lends itself to creating more verses. After children have learned the poem and have a feeling for the rhythm and pattern of repetition and rhyme, you could ask them to work as partners or in trios, creating a verse using a theme (such as kitchen utensils or food). They can take turns performing their creations.

The Animal Fair

I went to the animal fair

The birds and the beasts were there.

The big baboon by the light of the moon

Was combing his auburn hair.

The monkey bumped the skunk,

And sat on the elephant's trunk;

The elephant sneezed and fell to his knees,

And that was the end of the monk,

The monk, the monk, the monk,

The monk, the monk, the monk.

SUGGESTION: Children will enjoy the funny images in this traditional rhyme. Move along at a good pace and have them think of different ways to perform it. For example, they could clap and get louder on the last three lines or could let their voices slowly dwindle to a whisper on the last line. Alternatively, some children can softly and rhythmically chant *the monk* throughout the song while others sing or chant the lines, joining in unison on the last two.

Apples Are Red

Apples are red,

My nose is blue,

Standing at the bus stop,

Waiting for you.

SUGGESTION: Children might want to talk about why the speaker's nose might be blue and discuss the importance of being on time. They can speculate whether the speaker is waiting for the person or the bus.

Apples, Peaches

Apples, peaches,

Pears, plums,

Tell me when your

Birthday comes.

SUGGESTION: You can turn this chant into a game that children can play in small groups. One child begins by chanting and then pointing to another child and guessing the month of that child's birthday. If it is a correct guess, they exchange places and the new child repeats the process. As it continues, the game becomes more of a test of memory. This familiar chant is also a simple model to use when beginning to talk about adding *s* and *es* to make plurals.

As I Was Going to Banbury

As I was going to Banbury,

All on a summer's day,

My wife had butter, eggs, and cheese,

And I had corn and hay.

Bob drove the cows and Tom the swine,

Dick led the foal and mare.

I sold them all, then home again,

We came from Banbury fair.

SUGGESTION: After children have heard or recited the words several times, this rhyme provides a great opportunity to focus on rhythm. As you or a child read the words, have the group tap the rhythm using their finger on the table (or clap the syllables to begin) as a way to recognize and use the cadence.

At the Seaside

by Robert Louis Stevenson

When I was down beside the sea,

A wooden spade they gave to me

To dig the sandy shore.

My holes were empty like a cup.

In every hole the sea came up

Till it could come no more.

SUGGESTION: Spend some time talking about the meaning of the poem and mentally picturing the empty holes gradually filling up with seawater. Some children may not understand the concept that the water is under the sand and seeps in.

At the Zoo

by William Makepeace Thackeray

First I saw the white bear, then I saw the black;

Then I saw the camel with a hump upon his back;

Then I saw the gray wolf, with mutton in his maw;

Then I saw the wombat waddle in the straw;

Then I saw the elephant a-waving of his trunk;

Then I saw the monkeys—mercy, how unpleasantly they—stunk!

Autumn Leaves

Autumn leaves are falling, falling, falling.

Autumn leaves are spinning, spinning, spinning.

Autumn leaves are floating, floating, floating.

Autumn leaves are turning, turning, turning.

Autumn leaves are dancing, dancing, dancing.

Autumn leaves are blowing, blowing, blowing.

Autumn leaves are falling, falling, falling.

Autumn leaves are sleeping, sleeping, sleeping.

SUGGESTION: Children enjoy acting this out. Additionally, they can use the predictable pattern *Autumn leaves are* to create their own descriptive lines of poetry and prose. Pair this poem with Lois Ehlert's "Red Leaf, Yellow Leaf." They can also talk about how the repetition makes the poem more effective; for example, they could say it without repeating the last word in each line and compare the versions.

Away Down East

Away down east, away down west,

Away down Alabama,

The only girl that I like best,

Her name is Susie Anna.

I took her to a ball one night

And sat her down to supper.

The table fell and she fell too

And stuck her nose in the butter.

The butter, the butter,

The yellow margarine.

Two black eyes and a jelly nose

And all the rest turned green.

SUGGESTION: Divide the children into three groups and have each group read a verse. This is a good poem to use when trying to locate two-, three-, and four-syllable words all on one page.

fold
here

41

Bat, Bat

Bat, bat, come under my hat,

And I'll give you a slice of bacon.

And when I bake,

I'll give you a cake,

If I am not mistaken.

SUGGESTION: This poem has infectious rhymes and humorous imagery. Invite the children to substitute other *b* words for *bat*, such as *bird* or *butterfly*—or *bumblebee*! Because it is short and familiar, it's a perfect rhyme to revisit when children are working on distinguishing short and long *a* sounds.

The Bear

The other day   (The other day)
I met a bear,   (I met a bear,)
Away up there,   (Away up there,)
A great big bear!   (A great big bear!)

The other day I met a bear, away up there, a great big bear!

He looked at me,   (He looked at me,)
I looked at him.   (I looked at him.)
He sized up me,   (He sized up me,)
I sized up him.   (I sized up him.)

He looked at me, I looked at him. He sized up me, I sized up him.

And so I ran   (And so I ran)
Away from there.   (Away from there.)
And right behind   (And right behind)
Me was that bear.   (Me was that bear.)

And so I ran away from there. And right behind me was that bear.

Ahead of me   (Ahead of me)
I saw a tree,   (I saw a tree,)
A great big tree,   (A great big tree,)
Oh, golly gee!   (Oh, golly gee!)

Ahead of me I saw a tree, a great big tree, oh, golly gee!

continued

SUGGESTION: This poem uses an echo technique; words and phrases repeat throughout this story about a meeting with a bear. This is a good poem for English-language learners. Children can listen to and repeat one line at a time. And then everyone in unison repeats each four-line stanza as one line.

The lowest branch   (The lowest branch)
Was ten feet up.   (Was ten feet up.)
I had to jump   (I had to jump)
And trust my luck.   (And trust my luck.)

The lowest branch was ten feet up,
I had to jump and trust my luck.

And so I jumped   (And so I jumped)
Into the air,   (Into the air,)
And missed that branch   (And missed that branch)
Away up there.   (Away up there.)

And so I jumped into the air,
And missed that branch away up there.

Now don't you fret,   (Now don't you fret,)
And don't you frown.   (And don't you frown.)
I caught that branch   (I caught that branch)
On the way back down.   (On the way back down.)

Now don't you fret, and don't you frown.
I caught that branch on the way back down.

That's all there is,   (That's all there is,)
There is no more,   (There is no more,)
Until I meet   (Until I meet)
That bear once more.   (That bear once more.)

That's all there is, there is no more,
Until I meet that bear once more.

Bears Eat Honey

Bears eat honey.

Cows eat corn.

What do you eat

When you get up in the morn?

Monkeys eat bananas.

Cows eat corn.

What do you eat

When you get up in the morn?

Horses eat oats.

Cows eat corn.

What do you eat

When you get up in the morn?

SUGGESTION: Ask your class what different animals eat and what their own favorite foods are. List these foods and then read them over together. Children may add new food verses after they have learned the poem.

Bed in Summer

by Robert Louis Stevenson

In winter I get up at night

And dress by yellow candlelight.

In summer, quite the other way,

I have to go to bed by day.

I have to go to bed and see

The birds still hopping on the tree,

Or hear the grown-up people's feet

Still going past me in the street.

And does it not seem hard to you,

When all the sky is clear and blue,

And I should like so much to play,

To have to go to bed by day?

SUGGESTION: Many children will agree with the last stanza. Read this poem aloud several times and then return to each stanza asking children to discuss and explain what the poet meant. You may get into a discussion of the fact that days are so much longer in summer.

Bees

A swarm of bees in May,

Is worth a load of hay.

A swarm of bees in June,

Is worth a silver spoon.

A swarm of bees in July,

Isn't worth a fly.

SUGGESTION: After children are familiar with the words, encourage them to think about various ways to perform this verse. They could recite it as one group; they could divide into two groups and alternate lines, or they could become three groups and each group recites a couplet. Farm wisdom is being passed on in this verse. What could the farmer mean by these observations? What's a swarm of bees worth in March or…?

fold
here

47

Betty Botter

Betty Botter bought some butter,

"But," she said, "this butter's bitter;

If I put it in my batter,

It will make my batter bitter.

But a bit of better butter

Will make my batter better."

So she bought a bit of butter

Better than her bitter butter,

And she put it in her batter.

So 'twas better Betty Botter

Bought a bit of better butter.

SUGGESTION: Some students, especially if they are learning English, may need a little help with some of these words, such as *batter* and *bitter*. Children love to say this verse slowly the first time, and then increase their speed on subsequent readings—trying not to mispronounce the words! This is a great poem to use as children learn to identify short vowel sounds. And be sure to revisit this again when focusing on double consonants in the middle of words.

Big Ship Sailing

There's a big ship sailing on the illy ally oh,

Illy ally oh, illy ally oh.

There's a big ship sailing on the illy ally oh,

Hi, ho, illy ally oh.

There's a big ship sailing, rocking on the sea,

Rocking on the sea, rocking on the sea.

There's a big ship sailing, rocking on the sea,

Hi, ho, rocking on the sea.

There's a big ship sailing back again,

Back again, back again.

There's a big ship sailing back again,

Hi, ho, back again.

SUGGESTION: Children love to sing this as they follow a leader in and out and around the room, down the "alley alley oh." Everyone *toots* and *salutes* as the ship leaves the "dock." Help children make up additional verses of this song featuring other kinds of boats and ships and appropriate descriptive words: tugboats chugging, sailboats tacking, fireboats standing by, etc. Note: This song is featured on John Langstaff's CD *Songs for Singing Children*.

Birds of a Feather

Birds of a feather flock together

And so do pigs and swine.

Rats and mice will have their choice,

And so will I have mine.

SUGGESTION: This seemingly simple verse has a deeper meaning. After children have heard these words, and read them together, help them reflect on what they could mean.

Bow-wow, Says the Dog

Bow-wow, says the dog;
Mew, mew, says the cat;
Grunt, grunt goes the hog;
And squeak, goes the rat.

Chirp, chirp, says the sparrow;
Caw, caw, says the crow;
Quack, quack, says the duck;
And what cuckoos say, you know.

So, with sparrows and cuckoos,
With rats and with dogs,
With ducks and with crows,
With cats and with hogs.

A fine song I have made,
To please you, my dear;
And if it's well sung,
'Twill be charming to hear.

SUGGESTION: You can assign children to make the animal sounds in the poem as well as choose the narrator. And the last few lines offer an opportunity to discuss having fun with the noise while also being "charming to hear." After they have become familiar with the words, it is a great poem to revisit when you are dealing with *ou*, *ow*, and *aw* vowel combinations.

The Boy Stood in the Supper-room

The boy stood in the supper-room

Whence all but he had fled;

He'd eaten seven pots of jam

And he was gorged with bread.

"Oh, one more crust before I bust!"

He cried in accents wild;

He licked the plates, he sucked the spoons—

He was a vulgar child.

There came a burst of thunder-sound—

The boy—Oh! Where was he?

Ask of the maid who mopped him up,

The bread crumbs and the tea!

SUGGESTION: Children will probably need to hear this poem a few times before it makes sense. Teach students that this is a "cautionary tale." What does it warn them about? Pairing this poem with Maurice Sendak's book *Pierre: A Cautionary Tale in Five Acts and a Prologue* will give children another experience with the genre.

Bring the Wagon Home, John

Oh, bring the wagon home, John,

It will not hold us all.

We used to ride around in it,

When you and I were small.

SUGGESTION: Children can discuss why the speaker wants to keep the wagon even though she (or he) and John have out-grown it. They might talk about toys that they have kept even though they are too old for them.

The Brook

Grumbling, stumbling,

Fumbling all the day;

Fluttering, stuttering,

Muttering away;

Rustling, hustling,

Rustling as it flows;

This is how the brook talks,

Bubbling as it goes.

SUGGESTION: Ask a few children to say the word *bubbling* repeatedly while others read the verse.

Buffalo Gals

As I was walking down the street,
Down the street, down the street,
A pretty little gal I chanced to meet,
Oh, she was fair to see.

Refrain

> Buffalo Gals, won't you come out tonight,
> Come out tonight, come out tonight?
> Buffalo Gals, won't you come out tonight,
> And dance by the light of the moon?

I stopped her and we had a talk,
Had a talk, had a talk,
Her feet took up the whole sidewalk,
And left no room for me.

Refrain

I asked her if she'd have a dance,
Have a dance, have a dance,
I thought that I might have a chance,
To shake a foot with her.

Refrain

I danced with a gal with a hole in her stocking,
And her heel kept a-knocking, and her toes kept a-rocking.
I danced with a gal with a hole in her stocking,
And we danced by the light of the moon.

Refrain

SUGGESTION: Have the children sing this rhythmic song while one child shakes a tambourine during the refrain. Ask children to notice the rhyming pattern of the verses and refrain.

Bullfrog

Here's Mr. Bullfrog,

Sitting on a rock.

Along comes _____.

Mr. Bullfrog jumps, KERPLOP!

SUGGESTION: *Kerplop* is the favorite word in this poem. Children enjoy reciting the verse, inserting names of classmates or others, and jumping off imaginary rocks as they shout, "KERPLOP!" This simple verse is fun to revisit when you begin discussing abbreviations. You can add Mr. or Ms. and the child's surname as a way to add them to the poem with Mr. Bullfrog.

Bunnies' Bedtime

"My bunnies must go to bed,"

The little mother rabbit said.

"But I will count them first to see

If they have all come back to me.

One bunny, two bunnies, three bunnies dear,

Four bunnies, five bunnies—yes, all are here.

They are the prettiest things alive—

My bunnies, one, two, three, four, five."

SUGGESTION: Your children will enjoy substituting different animals, such as bears, kittens, or dogs.

The Bus

There is a painted bus,

With twenty painted seats,

It carries painted people

Along the painted streets.

They pull the painted bell,

The painted driver stops,

And they all get out together

At the little painted shops.

SUGGESTION: Help children understand that this poem describes a scene in a painting. Several children may volunteer to paint the scene. Make sure that every detail is included.

Buttercups and Daisies

Buttercups and daisies,

Oh what pretty flowers,

Coming in the springtime,

To tell of sunny hours!

While the trees are leafless,

While the fields are bare,

Buttercups and daisies,

Spring up everywhere.

SUGGESTION: Ask children to share with you what they know about flowers. How many kinds can they think of? Make a class list together. Illustrate the list, with the help of such picture books as *Allison's Zinnia*, by Anita Lobel; this ABC book has paintings of twenty-six different flowers.

fold
here

59

The Butterfly

April

Come she will,

May

She will stay,

June

She'll change her tune,

July

She will fly,

August

Die she must.

SUGGESTION: Point out the unique structure of this poem with one-word lines followed with a rhyming description. This poem indirectly suggests the life cycle of a butterfly from April to August. Children can talk about what each stage means (including *change her tune*, which means turning from a pupa to a butterfly). They may want to consult some informational books and produce drawings of each stage that can be illustrated by the poem.

Calico Pie

by Edward Lear

I

Calico pie,

The little birds fly

Down to the calico tree.

Their wings were blue,

And they sang "Tilly-loo!"

Till away they flew;

And they never came back to me!

They never came back,

They never came back,

They never came back to me!

II

Calico jam,

The little fish swam

Over the Syllabub Sea.

He took off his hat

To the Sole and the Sprat,

And the Willeby-wat;

But he never came back to me!

He never came back,

He never came back,

He never came back to me!

continued

SUGGESTION: Assign children to four groups. Each group can practice one section and perform it for their classmates. What would *calico* or *calico pie* be? Look up the word *calico* in the dictionary. Have children speculate on why Edward Lear used the word *calico* in the poem. They may have heard of a calico cat.

III

Calico ban,

The little Mice ran

To be ready in time for tea.

Flippity-flup,

They drank it all up,

And danced in the cup;

But they never came back to me!

They never came back,

They never came back,

They never came back to me!

IV

Calico drum,

The Grasshoppers come,

The Buttlerfly, Beetle, and Bee,

Over the ground,

Around and round,

With a hop and a bound;

But they never came back to me!

They never came back,

They never came back,

They never came back to me!

The Cat of Cats

by William Brighty Rands

I am the cat of cats. I am

The everlasting cat!

Cunning, and old, and sleek as jam,

The everlasting cat!

I hunt the vermin in the night—

The everlasting cat!

For I see best without the light—

The everlasting cat!

SUGGESTION: Children will enjoy this image of a cat. You may want to make a web of all the words describing the cat and discuss what the poet means by *everlasting cat.*

Caterpillar

by Christina Rossetti

Brown and furry

Caterpillar in a hurry,

Take your walk

To the shady leaf, or stalk,

Or what not,

Which may be the chosen spot.

No toad spy you,

Hovering bird of prey pass by you;

Spin and die,

To live again a butterfly.

SUGGESTION: The life cycle of a butterfly is a wonderful thing to know about and to recite together as a poem. Talk about the many descriptive images in this verse. You might consider presenting this with other poems such as "The Butterfly," "A Caterpillar Crawled," "Fuzzy Little Caterpillar," or "Little Arabella Miller" (found in this volume).

A Caterpillar Crawled

A caterpillar crawled

To the top of the tree.

"I think I'll take a nap," said he.

So under a leaf he began to creep

To spin his cocoon,

And he fell asleep.

All winter long he slept in his bed,

'Til spring came along one day and said,

"Wake up, wake up, little sleepyhead,

Wake up, it's time to get out of bed."

So he opened his eyes that sunshiny day.

Lo! He was a butterfly and flew away.

SUGGESTION: Show the children how to creep the first two fingers of one hand up their other arm as they say the first two lines and put one hand over the other during the rest of the first verse. For *wake up*, have them shake one hand; then have them lock their thumbs and wave the fingers of both hands as the butterfly flies away.

The Centipede's Song

Forty thousand little legs,

Walking down the stairs.

Forty thousand little feet,

Walking down in pairs.

Crunching on the gravel,

Marching in the shade,

Sounding like an army

Of soldiers on parade.

How happy are the centipedes,

Who do not have a care,

Except to keep their thousands

Of boots in good repair.

SUGGESTION: Children can discuss how the poem helps them appreciate this insect by comparing the centipede's feet to people's feet. It might also be interesting to look at the word *centipede* and connect it to other words like *pedal, pedestrian, pedestal, cent, century*, thinking about the parts of the words that look alike and also how they might be connected by meaning.

The Chickens

Said the first little chicken,
With a queer little squirm,
"I wish I could find
A fat little worm."

Said the next little chicken,
With an odd little shrug,
"I wish I could find
A fat little slug."

Said the third little chicken,
With a sharp little squeal,
"I wish I could find
Some nice yellow meal."

Said the fourth little chicken,
With a small sigh of grief,
"I wish I could find
A little green leaf."

Said the fifth little chicken,
With a faint little moan,
"I wish I could find
A wee gravel stone."

"Now, see here," said the mother,
From the green garden patch,
"If you want any breakfast,
Just come here and scratch."

SUGGESTION: As children become familiar with this poem, you can assign parts. The performers will need practice time to work with the language and remember their parts. Partners are assigned one stanza to rehearse together—one as narrator and one as the chicken for that particular verse. Then the six partner groups perform their stanzas in poem order. Don't miss the chance to revisit this poem when children are learning about words with vowels and *r*, as there are many examples here.

Choosing a Kitten

A black-nosed kitten will slumber all the day;

A white-nosed kitten is ever glad to play;

A yellow-nosed kitten will answer to your call;

And a gray-nosed kitten I like best of all.

SUGGESTION: Invite children to talk about their own pets, describe them, and tell how they picked them. Children who don't have pets may talk about pretend puppies, cuddly kittens, and other animals they wish they had. Attach children's written descriptions next to their artwork.

The City Mouse and the Garden Mouse

by Christina Rossetti

The city mouse lives in a house,

The garden mouse lives in a bower;

He's friendly with the frogs and toads,

And sees the pretty plants in flower.

The city mouse eats bread and cheese,

The garden mouse eats what he can;

We will not grudge him seeds and stalks,

Poor little, timid, furry man.

SUGGESTION: Discuss words like *bower, grudge,* and *timid,* which children may not know. After children have heard the poem, see if they can make some comparisons between the lives of the two very different mice. How would your class members like to live in a city? In a garden? Why?

Clouds

White sheep, white sheep,

On a blue hill.

When the wind stops,

You all stand still.

When the wind blows,

You walk away slow.

White sheep, white sheep

Where do you go?

SUGGESTION: Present this poem without the title and see if a discussion produces the *Clouds* as what the poem describes. Teach children about metaphor—using descriptive words to make comparisons, as this poem does. What are their thoughts about comparing clouds? Sponge-painted or torn-paper clouds are a great follow-up to learning this poem. Children's ideas, art, and language will be stimulated by a trip outside to look at clouds and find shapes in them.

Cockles and Mussels

In Dublin's fair city
Where girls are so pretty,
'Twas there I first met with
Sweet Molly Malone.

She drove a wheelbarrow
Through streets broad and narrow,
Crying, "Cockles and mussels,
Alive, alive-o."

Alive, alive-o
Alive, alive-o
Crying, "Cockles and mussels,
Alive, alive-o."

She was a fishmonger,
But sure 'twas no wonder,
For so were her mother
And father before.

They drove their wheelbarrows
Through streets broad and narrow.
Crying, "Cockles and mussels,
Alive, alive-o."

Alive, alive-o
Alive, alive-o
Crying, "Cockles and mussels,
Alive, alive-o."

SUGGESTION: Children will find it interesting to imagine a *fishmonger* selling live shellfish on the city streets and think about the rhythmic chant that served as advertising. If they are not near a seacoast town, you can tell them that this still happens today in areas near wharves.

The Codfish

The codfish lays ten thousand eggs,

The homely hen lays one.

The codfish never cackles

To tell you what she's done.

And so we scorn the codfish,

While the humble hen we prize,

Which only goes to show you

That it pays to advertise.

SUGGESTION: Have children discuss what makes this poem funny and uncover the comparisons in it. *It pays to advertise* is a common saying, but the humor lies in the comparison of the hen's cackle to television and newspaper ads.

Combinations

A flea flew by a bee. The bee

To flee the flea flew by a fly.

The fly flew high to flee the bee

Who flew to flee the flea who flew

To flee the fly who now flew by.

The bee flew by the fly. The fly

To flee the bee flew by the flea.

The flea flew high to flee the fly

Who flew to flee the bee who flew

To flee the flea who now flew by.

The fly flew by the flea. The flea

To flee the fly flew by the bee.

The bee flew high to flee the flea

Who flew to flee the fly who flew

To flee the bee who now flew by.

continued

continued

SUGGESTION: This tongue twister is a tough one, but the simple words make it easier for children to reread and practice. You might consider sharing only the first verse to get started. Keeping the first verse on a chart as a model, you could then substitute words into the repetitive pattern using cards on words or another chart. When children are familiar with the structure, give them a photocopy with all the verses, and they can practice reading the substitutions.

The flea flew by the fly. The fly

To flee the flea flew by the bee.

The bee flew high to flee the fly

Who flew to flee the flea who flew

To flee the bee who now flew by.

The fly flew by the bee. The bee

To flee the fly flew by the flea.

The flea flew high to flee the bee

Who flew to flee the fly who flew

To flee the flea who now flew by.

The bee flew by the flea. The flea

To flee the bee flew by the fly.

The fly flew high to flee the flea

Who flew to flee the bee who flew

To flee the fly who now flew by.

The Cow

by Robert Louis Stevenson

The friendly cow, all red and white,

I love with all my heart;

She gives me cream with all her might,

To eat with apple-tart.

She wanders lowing here and there,

And yet she cannot stray,

All in the pleasant open air,

The pleasant light of day;

And blown by all the winds that pass

And wet with all the showers,

She walks among the meadow grass

And eats the meadow flowers.

SUGGESTION: Groups of children may take turns reading each verse of this poem. Ask children what they know about cows. Children can discuss how the milk from cows gives us butter and cream. Although many may not have seen a cow, they may understand that cows give milk and make sounds. Explain that *lowing* means the same as saying *moo*. Have them think about a cow's life, always walking through a meadow. There are many picture books about these animals: *The Cow Who Wouldn't Come Down*, by Paul Johnson, and *Cows in the Kitchen*, by June Crebbin.

fold here

Cradle Song

by Alfred, Lord Tennyson

What does little birdie say
In her nest at peep of day?
Let me fly, says little birdie,
Mother, let me fly away.
Birdie, rest a little longer,
Till the little wings are stronger;
So she rests a little longer,
Then she flies away.

What does little baby say,
In her bed at peep of day?
Baby says, like little birdie,
Let me rise and fly away.
Baby, sleep a little longer,
Till the little limbs are stronger;
If she sleeps a little longer,
Baby too shall fly away.

SUGGESTION: This poem is about growth and change. Help children understand why Tennyson is comparing a baby with a small bird. They may want to talk about how children and birds are alike but also how they are different in terms of the growth cycle.

The Cupboard

by Walter de la Mare

I know a little cupboard,
With a teeny tiny key,
And there's a jar of Lollipops
For me, me, me.

It has a little shelf, my dear,
As dark as dark can be,
And there's a dish of Banbury Cakes
For me, me, me.

I have a small fat grandmamma,
With a very slippery knee,
And she's Keeper of the Cupboard,
With key, key, key.

And when I'm very good, my dear,
As good as good can be,
There's Banbury Cakes and Lollipops
For me, me, me.

SUGGESTION: Children will enjoy the repetition on the last line of each stanza. They can substitute other treats for
Lollipops and *Banbury Cakes*, or they may enjoy making an artistic collage by designing lollipops with colorful patterns
covered with a cardboard "door."

Curly Locks

Curly Locks, Curly Locks,

Will you be mine?

You shall not wash dishes,

Nor yet feed the swine,

But sit on a cushion

And sew a fine seam;

And feed upon strawberries,

Sugar, and cream.

SUGGESTION: Be sure that children know that *locks* means *hair* and *swine* means *pigs*. Have one small group read the first
two lines and all children read the last six lines.

Daffy Down Dilly

Daffy Down Dilly

Has come to town,

In a yellow petticoat,

And a green gown.

SUGGESTION: Children will enjoy the simplicity of this poem but may need some discussion to understand the metaphor. Discuss the daffodil as one of the signs of spring. If you have flowers in the classroom or a view of flowers, this is a good poem to place near them or on a window.

fold here

79

December Leaves

by Kaye Starbird

The fallen leaves are cornflakes

That fill the lawn's wide dish,

And night and noon

The wind's a spoon

That stirs them with a swish.

The sky's a silver sifter

A-sifting white and slow,

That gently shakes

On crisp brown flakes

The sugar known as snow.

SUGGESTION: Enjoy the descriptive language of this poem with your class. Glue green, gold, and orange *cornflake leaves* onto a chart of the poem. (Make the leaves by mixing one or two tablespoons of rubbing alcohol and some food coloring in a large plastic bag, adding cornflakes, and then closing and shaking the bag.) Add silver glitter for the snow.

Denise Sees the Fleece

Denise sees the fleece,

Denise sees the fleas.

At least Denise could sneeze,

And feed and freeze the fleas.

SUGGESTION: This nonsense verse is enjoyable because of the juxtaposition of words that sound the same (or almost the same) but mean completely different things. After children know the poem, you may want to revisit it for examples of *ee* and *ea* words.

fold
here

81

Do Your Ears Hang Low?

Do your ears hang low?

Do they wobble to and fro?

Can you tie them in a knot?

Can you tie them in a bow?

Can you throw them o'er your shoulder,

Like a Continental Soldier?

Do your ears hang low?

Do your ears hang high?

Do they reach up to the sky?

Do they wrinkle when they're wet?

Do they straighten when they're dry?

Can you wave them at your neighbor,

With an element of flavor?

Do your ears hang high?

continued

SUGGESTION: One popular way to sing this song is to take one stanza and sing it over and over, speeding up each time, until it is no longer possible to go faster. Use hand motions to imitate the ears and other parts of the body while singing or chanting.

Do your ears hang wide?

Do they flap from side to side?

Do they wave in the breeze,

From the slightest little sneeze?

Can you soar above the nation,

With a feeling of elation?

Do your ears hang wide?

Do your ears fall off,

When you give a great big cough?

Do they lie there on the ground,

Or bounce up at every sound?

Can you stick them in your pocket,

Just like Davy Crockett?

Do your ears fall off?

ADDITIONAL VERSES:

Does your tongue hang down?
Does it flop all around?
Is it stringy at the bottom?
Is it curly at the top?
Can you use it for a swatter?
Can you use it for a blotter?
Does your tongue hang down?

Does your nose hang low?
Does your nose hang low?
Can you flap it up and down
As you fly around the town?
Can you turn it up for sure
When you hear an awful bore?
Does your nose hang low?

Do your eyes pop out?
Do they bounce all about?
Can you use them like a ball?
Can you take them in and out?
Can they do the boogie woogie
Like they do in any movie?
Do your eyes pop out?

Doctor Foster

Doctor Foster

Went to Gloucester

In a shower of rain.

He stepped in a puddle

Right up to his middle

And never went there again.

SUGGESTION: Be sure children know that *Gloucester* may not look it but rhymes with *Foster.* You may want to use this song on a rainy day or tape it on the window.

Donkey, Donkey

Donkey, donkey, old and gray,

Open your mouth and gently bray.

Lift your ears and blow your horn,

To wake the world this sleepy morn.

Gee up, donkey, to the fair.

What shall I buy when I get there?

A half-penny apple, a penny pear,

Gee up, donkey, to the fair.

Donkey, donkey, do not bray,

But mend your pace and trot away.

Indeed, the market's almost done,

My butter's melting in the sun.

SUGGESTION: Ask children to suggest actions to accompany the poem. They will enjoy *opening their mouth to bray* and *blowing their horn to wake the world*. Children can talk about past times when people rode donkeys, mules, or horses to market and home again. Children may understand *market* as grocery store and *fair* as a carnival, but in history they were more similar in that people would go to sell and buy things. They can retell this poem in prose, noting the sequence of events.

fold
here

85

The Donut Song

Oh, I ran around the corner,

And I ran around the block

I ran right in to the baker's shop.

I grabbed me a donut,

Right out of the grease,

And I handed the lady,

A five-cent piece.

She looked at the nickel,

And she looked at me.

She said, "This nickel,

Is no good to me.

There's a hole in the nickel,

And it goes right through."

Said I, "There's a hole in your donut, too!

Thanks for the donut. Good-bye!"

SUGGESTION: These words may be sung to the tune of "Turkey in the Straw." Or children may choose to recite the song as a "rap." It might be fun to experiment with both things happening at once: a "rap" against the background of a sung version.

Doodle-lee-do

Please sing to me that sweet melody,
Called Doodle-lee-do-doodle-lee-do.
I like the rest, but the one I like best,
Goes Doodle-lee-do-doodle-lee-do.

It's the simplest thing, there isn't much to it.
All you gotta do is Doodle-lee-do it.
I like it so that wherever I go,
It's the Doodle-lee-doodle-lee-do.

Come on and Waddle-lee-atcha-waddle-lee-atcha,
Waddle-lee-o-waddle-lee-o.
Waddle-lee-atcha-waddle-lee-atcha,
Waddle-lee-o-waddle-lee-o.

It's the simplest thing, there isn't much to it.
All you gotta do is Doodle-lee-do it.
I like it so that wherever I go,
It's the Doodle-lee-doodle-lee-do.

SUGGESTION: Hand movements go with this funny song. Sit down to do it. In rhythm with the song follow this sequence: (1) slap hands on thighs twice; (2) pass hands (palms down) over each other twice; (3) snap both fingers three times (on *doodle-lee-doo*); (4) raise arms high and snap both fingers three more times (on second *doodle-lee-do*). Keep repeating for stanzas one, two, and four. On third stanza, continuously slap thighs on *come on and*. Then speed up and roll hands snapping fingers three times again on *waddle-lee-o*.

Down by the Bay

Down by the bay where the watermelons grow,
Back to my home I dare not go.
For if I do my mother will say,
"Did you ever see a pig dancing the jig?"
Down by the bay.

Down by the bay where the watermelons grow,
Back to my home I dare not go.
For if I do my mother will say,
"Did you ever see a whale with a polka-dot tail?"
Down by the bay.

Down by the bay where the watermelons grow,
Back to my home I dare not go.
For if I do my mother will say,
"Did you ever see a bear combing his hair?"
Down by the bay.

Down by the bay where the watermelons grow,
Back to my home I dare not go.
For if I do my mother will say,
"Did you ever see a moose kissing a goose?"
Down by the bay.

Down by the bay where the watermelons grow,
Back to my home I dare not go.
For if I do my mother will say,
"Did you ever see a bee with a sunburned knee?"
Down by the bay.

SUGGESTION: Have children move along rapidly as they perform the poem, slowing down on the fifth line (*Down by the bay*) of each stanza, holding *down* for three counts. Children can create new verses with the same structure, for example, *Did you ever see a snake eating cake?*

Elephant

The elephant carries a great big trunk.

She never packs it with her clothes.

It has no lock and it has no key,

But she takes it wherever she goes.

SUGGESTION: This short verse plays on the word *trunk*. Explain to children the meaning of *pun* or *play on words*. If children draw cartoons illustrating this rhyme, the double meaning of the word will stick in their heads. Remember to return to this one when working on words with multiple meanings. Pair this, for a performance of elephants, with "The Elephant Goes Like This" (also in this volume). Assign groups to learn a verse so they can perform it for the rest of the class.

The Elephant Goes Like This

The elephant goes like this, like that.

He's terribly big, and he's terribly fat.

He has no fingers, he has no toes,

But goodness gracious, what a nose!

SUGGESTION: Children may want to do an "elephant walk" while saying the poem several times. The poem can be recited at a slow pace to time their steps. Pair this with the poem "The Elephant" (also in this volume.).

Eletelephony

by Laura E. Richards

Once there was an elephant,

Who tried to use the telephant—

No! No! I mean an elephone

Who tried to use the telephone—

(Dear me! I am not certain quite

That even now I've got it right.)

Howe'er it was, he got his trunk

Entangled in the telephunk;

The more he tried to get it free,

The louder buzzed the telephee—

(I fear I'd better drop the song

Of elephop and telephong!)

SUGGESTION: Children may want to illustrate this poem by drawing the elephant tangled in the telephone cord. Probably, they will see the cordless phone as a solution. After they know the poem, make a list of all the words and connections between the word parts. Have children practice this poem in order to correctly recite the word play presented.

Eye Rhymes

You see me, I see you.

Your eyes are blue. Mine are, too.

Your eyes are big and round and brown.

They must be the prettiest eyes in town.

When I look at you, know what I see?

Eyes as green as green can be.

Blue eyes, green eyes,

Brown eyes, hey.

Your eyes are gray,

And I like them that way.

SUGGESTION: Divide the class in half and have the two groups read every other verse, with everyone reading the final
verse. You could also divide the class by the color of their eyes and then have that particular group read the related lines.
Illustrate the poem by encircling it with portraits of people of every eye color.

Fiddle-i-fee

I had a cat and my cat pleased me.
I fed my cat under yonder tree.
Cat plays fiddle-i-fee.

I had a duck and my duck pleased me.
I fed my duck under yonder tree.
Duck plays quaa-quaa, quaa-quaa,
Cat plays fiddle-i-fee.

I had a goose and my goose pleased me.
I fed my goose under yonder tree.
Goose plays hum-sum, hum-sum,
Duck plays quaa-quaa, quaa-quaa,
Cat plays fiddle-i-fee.

ADDITIONAL VERSES:

I had hen and my hen pleased me.
I fed my hen under yonder tree.
Hen plays chimmy-chuck, chimmy-chuck,
etc.

I had a pig and my pig pleased me.
I fed my pig under yonder tree.
Pig plays griffy-griffy, griffy-griffy,
etc.

I had a cow and my cow pleased me.
I fed my cow under yonder tree.
Cow plays strum-strum, strum-strum,
etc.

I had a horse and my horse pleased me.
I fed my horse under yonder tree.
Horse plays dub-ub, dub-ub,
etc.

I had a dog and my dog pleased me.
I fed my dog under yonder tree.
Dog plays clickity-clack, clickity-clack,
etc.

I had a sheep and my sheep pleased me.
I fed my sheep under yonder tree.
Sheep plays shake-shake, shake-shake,
etc.

SUGGESTION: The numerous verses and cumulative structure of this verse may necessitate presenting it on chart paper or pocket chart to aid children in remembering. Your students may enjoy picking out interesting words and sounds, such as *griffy-griffy*, *chimmy-chuck*, and *fiddle-i-fee*.

"Fire! Fire!" Cried Mrs. McGuire!

"Fire! Fire!"
Cried Mrs. McGuire.
"Where? Where?"
Asked Mrs. Blair.
"All over town!"
Said Mrs. Brown.
"Get some water!"
Cried her daughter.
"We'd better jump!"
Said Mrs. Grump.
"That would be silly."
Replied Mrs. Minelli.
"What'll we do?"
Asked Mrs. LaRue.
"Turn in the alarm."
Said Mrs. Parm.
"Save us! Save us!"
Screamed Mrs. Davis.

The fire department
Got the call,
And the firemen saved them,
One and all!

SUGGESTION: Children can choose to take turns reading the dialogue of each character in this story poem. The whole group could read the last triumphant stanza. This poem is a great one to revisit when you are working with abbreviations. You can reread the poem substituting Mr., Ms., Dr., etc. To scaffold the learning of second-language students, use this poem with the picture book "*Fire! Fire!*" *Said Mrs. McGuire,* by Bill Martin Jr.

Firefighters

Up onto their loud, loud truck

The firefighters climb,

They're in an awful hurry,

They move in quick, quick time.

They're going to put out a fire,

Help is on the way.

They'll get there with their water hose

And spray and spray and spray.

SUGGESTION: Children will love to enact the part of firefighters. Ask them to add their own actions or movements as they recite. Pair this poem with Chris Demarest's alphabet book *Firefighters A to Z*.

fold
here

95

Five Cream Buns

Five cream buns in Teddy's shop,

Teddy's shop, Teddy's shop,

Five cream buns in Teddy's shop,

Round and fat with a cherry on top.

Along came _____,

Hungry one day,

She bought a cream bun

And took it away.

SUGGESTION: Make copies of this countdown poem and children can write in their own names. This poem and *Five Currant Buns* (see next page) are variations of each other. Be sure to call attention to this and use the opportunity to discuss *variations*. Children can compare the cadence and the syllable match of the lines. Working with a partner, or in small groups, encourage children to create their own variation. If the countdown structure of this poem is used as the model, children can create one stanza, reproduce their version for the class, and everyone can countdown the new versions together.

Five Currant Buns

Five currant buns in the baker's shop,
Big and round with some sugar on the top.
Along came Tom with a penny to pay,
Who bought a currant bun and took it right away.

Four currant buns in the baker's shop,
Big and round with some sugar on the top.
Along came Tom with a penny to pay,
Who bought a currant bun and took it right away.

Three currant buns in the baker's shop,
Big and round with some sugar on the top.
Along came Tom with a penny to pay,
Who bought a currant bun and took it right away.

Two currant buns in the baker's shop,
Big and round with some sugar on the top.
Along came Tom with a penny to pay,
Who bought a currant bun and took it right away.

One currant bun in the baker's shop,
Big and round with some sugar on the top.
Along came Tom with a penny to pay,
Who bought a currant bun and took it right away.

No currant buns in the baker's shop,
Big and round with some sugar on the top.
No one came with a penny to pay.
So close the baker's shop and have a baking day.

SUGGESTION: As you compare this variation to the previous poem, *Five Cream Buns*, be sure to note and discuss the difference in line presentation. The other variation is different in several small ways, including the visual presentation of the poem. It is presented in eight-line stanzas, whereas this one is presented on the page in four-line stanzas. Ask children to compare the poems, investigate the differences, and choose the model they'd like to use as they create new verses.

Five Fat Turkeys

Five fat turkeys are we.

We slept all night in a tree.

When the cook came around,

We couldn't be found.

So, that's why we're here, you see.

SUGGESTION: Children may already know this poem and the simple actions that go along: *holding five fingers up, putting the head to the side as if sleeping, shaking the head no, and pointing to themselves.* Because it is familiar, it is a great poem to revisit when reviewing contractions.

Five Little Owls

Five little owls in an old elm tree,

Fluffy and puffy as owls could be,

Blinking and winking with big round eyes

At the big round moon that hung in the skies:

As I passed beneath, I could hear one say,

"There'll be mouse for supper, there will, today!"

Then all of them hooted, "Tu-whit, Tu-whoo!

Yes, mouse for supper, Hoo hoo, Hoo hoo!"

SUGGESTION: You can vary the numbers—three, four, five owls. Have children say the verse once for each owl and have a different child say line six each time. This poem could lead to a discussion of owls as nocturnal creatures who like to hunt small rodents such as mice.

fold
here

99

Five Waiting Pumpkins

Five little pumpkins growing on a vine,

First one said, "It's time to shine!"

Second one said, "I love the fall!"

Third one said, "I'm round as a ball!"

Fourth one said, "I want to be a pie!"

Fifth one said, "Let's say good-bye!"

"Good-bye!" said one.

"Adios!" said two.

"Au revoir!" said three.

"Ciao!" said four.

"Aloha!" said five.

And five little pumpkins were picked that day!

SUGGESTION: When days grow cold and pumpkins make their appearance in markets, it's the perfect time to introduce this poem and discuss harvesting time. Reciting poems like this one just adds to the suspense. The pumpkins in this rhyme speak different languages. Invite your children to come up with other ways to say good-bye.

Fooba Wooba, John

Saw a flea kick a tree,
Fooba wooba, fooba wooba,
Saw a flea kick a tree,
Fooba wooba, John.
Saw a flea kick a tree,
In the middle of the sea,
Hey, John, ho, John,
Fooba wooba, John.

Saw a crow flying low,
Fooba wooba, fooba wooba,
Saw a crow flying low,
Fooba wooba, John.
Saw a crow flying low,
Miles and miles beneath the snow,
Hey, John, ho, John,
Fooba wooba, John.

Saw a bug give a shrug,
Fooba wooba, fooba wooba,
Saw a bug give a shrug,
Fooba wooba, John.
Saw a bug give a shrug,
In the middle of the rug,
Hey, John, ho, John,
Fooba wooba, John.

continued

SUGGESTION: This is an old camp song. Children can sing and act out the nonsense words (have them roll their arms around one another when they say *fooba wooba*). Use the following additional verses or create some *saw a, heard a, smelled a* verses together: *Saw a bee off to sea . . . With his fiddle across his knee. | Saw a bear scratch his ear . . .Wonderin' what we're doin' here. | Heard a cow say meow . . . And then take a little bow.*

Saw a whale chase a snail,
Fooba wooba, fooba wooba,
Saw a whale chase a snail,
Fooba wooba, John.
Saw a whale chase a snail,
All around a water pail.
Hey, John, ho, John,
Fooba wooba, John.

Saw two geese making cheese,
Fooba wooba, fooba wooba,
Saw two geese making cheese,
Fooba wooba, John.
Saw two geese making cheese,
One would hold and the other would squeeze,
Hey, John, ho, John,
Fooba wooba, John.

Saw a mule teaching school,
Fooba wooba, fooba wooba,
Saw a mule teaching school,
Fooba wooba, John.
Saw a mule teaching school,
To some bullfrogs in the pool,
Hey, John, ho, John,
Fooba wooba, John.

Found a Peanut

Found a peanut, found a peanut,
Found a peanut last night.
Last night I found a peanut,
Found a peanut last night.

Cracked it open, cracked it open,
Cracked it open last night.
Last night I cracked it open,
Cracked it open last night.

It was rotten, it was rotten,
It was rotten last night.
Last night it was rotten,
It was rotten last night.

Ate it anyway, ate it anyway,
Ate it anyway last night.
Last night ate it anyway,
Ate it anyway last night.

Got a tummy ache, got a tummy ache,
Got a tummy ache last night.
Last night got a tummy ache,
Got a tummy ache last night.

SUGGESTION: This song may be sung to the tune of "Clementine." The simple repetitive structure makes it easy for children to create additional verses…any phrase with three or four syllables should work. Point out the storytelling nature of the verses for children. Encourage them to continue the story as they make up verses or use: *Called the Doctor…*, *Penicillin…*, *Operation…*, *Was a Dream…*, *Then I Woke Up…*, and then back to *Found a Peanut…*

Four Seasons

Spring is showery, flowery, bowery.

Summer, hoppy, croppy, poppy.

Autumn, slippy, drippy, nippy.

Winter, breezy, sneezy, freezy.

SUGGESTION: Invite children to talk about how the words describe the seasons and why they might have been chosen. You may need to explain that *bower* refers to a garden arbor on which flowers grow.

The Fox Went Out on a
Chilly Night

The fox went out on a chilly night

He called to the moon to give him light.

For he'd many a mile to go that night

Before he'd reach the town-o, town-o, town-o.

He'd many a mile to go that night

Before he'd reach the town-o.

SUGGESTION: This old story song is a great one to use for line-up at the end of the day as children are getting ready to head out the door. You'll find it on many CDs and audiocassettes and in many picture books. One of them is Peter Spier's book *The Fox Went Out on a Chilly Night: An Old Song.*

fold
here

105

Frog Went A-courtin'

Frog went a-courtin' and he did ride.
Uh-huh; uh-huh.
Frog went a-courtin' and he did ride
With a sword and scabbard by his side.
Uh-huh; uh-huh.

He rode up to Miss Mousie's den.
Uh-huh; uh-huh.
He rode up to Miss Mousie's den,
Said "Please, Miss Mousie, won't you let me in?"
Uh-huh; uh-huh.

"First I must ask my Uncle Rat."
Uh-huh; uh-huh.
"First I must ask my Uncle Rat,
And see what he will say to that."
Uh-huh; uh-huh.

ADDITIONAL VERSES:

"Miss Mousie, won't you marry me?"
Uh-huh; uh-huh.
"Miss Mousie, won't you marry me,
Way down under the apple tree?"
Uh-huh; uh-huh.

"Where will the wedding supper be?"
Uh-huh; uh-huh.
"Where will the wedding supper be?
Under the same old apple tree?"
Uh-huh; uh-huh.

The first to come was a bumblebee.
Uh-huh; uh-huh.
The first to come was a bumblebee,
With a big bass fiddle on his knee.
Uh-huh; uh-huh.

The last to come was a mockingbird.
Uh-huh; uh-huh.
The last to come was a mockingbird,
Who said, "This marriage is absurd."
Uh-huh; uh-huh.

SUGGESTION: After children are familiar with the words, they might want to work in small groups to each practice a stanza for a whole class presentation. This song lends itself to making a class book or individual books with a stanza on each page. Children will enjoy making detailed illustrations for the scenes. John Langstaff has retold this story in a Caldecott Medal picture book of the same name. He sings the song on his CD *Songs for Singing Children.*

Fuzzy Little Caterpillar

Fuzzy little caterpillar,
Crawling, crawling on the ground,
Fuzzy little caterpillar,
Nowhere, nowhere to be found,
Though we've looked and looked and hunted,
Everywhere around!

When the little caterpillar
Found his furry coat too tight,
Then a snug cocoon he made him,
Spun of silk so soft and light,
Rolled himself away within it—
Slept there day and night.

See how this cocoon is stirring—
Now a little head we spy.
What! Is this our caterpillar,
Spreading gorgeous wings to dry?
Soon the free and happy creature
Flutters gaily by.

SUGGESTION: After children have listened to this poem and internalized the words, they can perform the finger play actions. They wiggle their thumbs to show the caterpillar crawling and then hide their thumbs (caterpillars) in a fist (cocoon) for the first two verses. For the third verse, they cross their thumbs and spread their fingers to show the butterfly drying its wings. Finally they wiggle their fingers to show the fluttering creatures.

The Goat

There was a man—now please take note—

There was a man who had a goat

He loved that goat—indeed he did—

He loved that goat, just like a kid.

One day that goat felt frisky and fine,

Ate three red shirts from off the line.

The man, he grabbed him by the back

And tied him to a railroad track.

But when the train drove into sight,

The goat grew pale and green with fright.

He heaved a sigh as if in pain,

Coughed up those shirts, and flagged the train.

SUGGESTION: This is often presented as an echo song with the leader reciting one line at a time and the group repeats the line. Discuss how *flagging* the train means stopping it.

Going on a Bear Hunt

Would you like to go on a bear hunt?
Okay—all right—come on—let's go!
Open the gate—close the gate. (*Clap hands*)

Coming to a bridge—can't go over it—can't go under it.
Let's cross it. (*Thump chest with fists*)

Coming to a river—can't go over it—can't go under it.
Let's swim it. (*Make swimming motions*)

Coming to a tree—can't go over it—can't go under it.
Let's climb it. (*Make climbing-up motions*)

No bears! (*Make climbing-down motions*)

Coming to a wheat field—can't go over it—can't go under it.
Let's go through it! (*Rub palms together to make swishing noise*)

Oh! Oh! I see a cave—it's dark in here. (*Cover eyes*)
I see two eyes—I feel something furry. (*Reach out hand*)

It's a bear!
Let's go home! (*Run in place*)

(*Quickly repeat the above actions in reverse order*)

Slam the gate! (*Clap hands*)
We made it!

SUGGESTION: Children will enjoy having a reproduced version of this poem. which is a favorite action rhyme. Concentration is required to do the motions rapidly in reverse order at thc cnd. They also will enjoy gluing verses into an eight-page book. A picture book, *We're Going on a Bear Hunt,* by Helen Oxenbury, is a favorite illustrated version.

Gold Ships

There are gold ships.

There are silver ships.

But there's no ship

Like a friendship.

SUGGESTION: Explore the meaning of this poem with a good discussion. Children enjoy puzzling things like this out.

Golden Slumbers

Golden slumbers kiss your eyes,

Smiles awake you when you rise.

Sleep, pretty baby, do not cry,

And I will sing a lullaby.

Rock then, rock then, lullaby.

ADDITIONAL VERSE:
Care is heavy, therefore sleep you,
You are care, and care must keep you.
Sleep, pretty baby, do not cry,
And I will sing a lullaby.
Rock then, rock then, lullaby.

SUGGESTION: Invite some children to hum softly while the others read the verse.

Good, Better, Best

Good, better, best,

Never let it rest,

Till your good is better

And your better, best.

SUGGESTION: This poem has a moral lesson and is a good motto for children. They can discuss the meaning in terms of doing their personal best each day. Post it in the classroom.

Good Morning, Merry Sunshine!

Good morning, merry sunshine!

How did you wake so soon?

You've scared the little stars away,

And shined away the moon.

I saw you go to sleep last night

Before I stopped my playing.

How did you get way over there,

And where have you been staying?

I never go to sleep, dear one,

I just go round to see

My little children of the

East who rise and watch for me.

I waken all the birds and bees

And flowers on my way.

And now come back to see the child

Who stayed out late to play.

SUGGESTION: This poem is a good example of personification. It may take children a while to figure out the real meaning of the poem. Enjoy the language and talk about how the moon or stars could also be described so that they seem like people.

The Greedy Man

The greedy man is he who sits

And bites bits out of plates,

Or else takes up a calendar

And gobbles all the dates.

SUGGESTION: Children will enjoy acting out this funny poem with its images of the greedy man gobbling *bits of plates* and *calendar dates.* This is a fun poem to revisit when children are identifying long and short vowel sounds in words.

The Greengrocer's Love Song

Do you carrot all for me?

My heart beets for you.

With your turnip nose

And your radish face

You are a peach.

If we cantaloupe

Lettuce marry.

Weed make a swell pear.

SUGGESTION: This poem plays with language in a way children will enjoy. They may need some discussion to understand how the names of fruits and vegetables have been used to represent messages (*If we cantaloupe* equals *If we can't elope*).

fold
here

115

Gregory Griggs

Gregory Griggs, Gregory Griggs,

Had twenty-seven different wigs.

He wore them up, he wore them down,

To please the people of the town.

He wore them east, he wore them west,

But he never could tell which he loved the best.

SUGGESTION: This poem has a good infectious beat. Children will enjoy saying the poem together and writing about Gregory Griggs. Why *does* he have twenty-seven wigs? Collect children's drawings to make a mural or poetry chart to show off Gregory Griggs and all those hairpieces.

Happy Thought

by Robert Louis Stevenson

The world is so full

Of a number of things,

I'm sure we should all

Be as happy as kings.

SUGGESTION: Collect happy thoughts to draw and share after enjoying the poem together. This could become an ongoing "Happy Thoughts" list—a handy addition to a classroom bulletin board.

Hickety, Pickety

Hickety, pickety, my black hen.

She lays eggs for gentlemen.

Sometimes nine,

And sometimes ten.

Hickety, pickety, my black hen.

SUGGESTION: Children will easily recall this simple poem. The rhythm is infectious. It's hard to get the words out of your head. Revisit this one when discussing compound words.

Higgledy, Piggledy, See How They Run

by Kate Greenaway

Higgledy, piggledy, see how they run!

Hopperty, popperty! What is the fun?

Has the sun or the moon tumbled into the sea?

What is the matter, now? Pray tell it me!

Higgledy, piggledy, how can I tell?

Hopperty, popperty! Hark the bell!

The rats and the mice even scamper away;

Who can say what may not happen today?

SUGGESTION: There is a dangerous secret hidden in this poem: What is going on here? What does the bell have to do with this poem? And *where* is it? Children should be able to work together or in small groups to figure out the meaning and then share it with the whole class.

The Hobbyhorse

I had a little hobbyhorse,

And it was dapple gray.

Its head was made of pea-straw,

Its tail was made of hay.

I sold it to an old woman

For a dollar bill.

And I'll not sing my song again

Till everything is still.

SUGGESTION: This is a fun poem to do around the circle. In groups of eight, assign each child one line (with groups of four—assign lines one and five; two and six; etc.). Facing each other, each child recites his or her lines followed by the next child in the circle. During practice, children will undoubtedly increase the pace and have fun making it a line-by-line race around the circle. Afterward, have them work to keep the rhythm and cadence of the performance smooth—almost as if one person was reciting. Revisit this poem when children are working with vowel sounds represented by different patterns in words (*a–e, ay, ai*).

The House That Jack Built

This is the house that Jack built.

This is the malt
That lay in the house that Jack built.

This is the rat,
That ate the malt,
That lay in the house that Jack built.

This is the cat,
That killed the rat,
That ate the malt,
That lay in the house that Jack built.

This is the dog,
That worried the cat,
That killed the rat,
That ate the malt,
That lay in the house that Jack built.

This is the cow with the crumpled horn,
That tossed the dog,
That worried the cat,
That killed the rat,
That ate the malt,
That lay in the house that Jack built.

continued

SUGGESTION: This old story poem is cumulative. The repeating lines in each stanza help children learn the words. Explain that *malt* is grain. Children may think of ideas to create their own cumulative verse, such as *This is the castle that Maria built.*

This is the maiden all forlorn,
That milked the cow with the crumpled horn,
That tossed the dog,
That worried the cat,
That killed the rat,
That ate the malt,
That lay in the house that Jack built.

This is the man all tattered and torn,
That kissed the maiden all forlorn,
That milked the cow with the crumpled horn,
That tossed the dog,
That worried the cat,
That killed the rat,
That ate the malt,
That lay in the house that Jack built.

This is the leader all shaven and shorn,
That married the man all tattered and torn,
That kissed the maiden all forlorn,
That milked the cow with the crumpled horn,
That tossed the dog,
That worried the cat,
That killed the rat,
That ate the malt,
That lay in the house that Jack built.

continued

This is the rooster that crowed in the morn,
That woke the leader all shaven and shorn,
That married the man all tattered and torn,
That kissed the maiden all forlorn,
That milked the cow with the crumpled horn,
That tossed the dog,
That worried the cat,
That killed the rat,
That ate the malt,
That lay in the house that Jack built.

This is the farmer sowing his corn,
That kept the rooster that crowed in the morn,
That woke the leader all shaven and shorn,
That married the man all tattered and torn,
That kissed the maiden all forlorn,
That milked the cow with the crumpled horn,
That tossed the dog,
That worried the cat,
That killed the rat,
That ate the malt,
That lay in the house that Jack built.

How Many Miles to Babylon?

How many miles to Babylon?

Threescore miles and ten.

Can I get there by candlelight?

Yes, and back again.

If your heels are nimble and light,

You may get there by candlelight.

SUGGESTION: There is a quiet, hushed feeling associated with this poem. Talk to children about this mood and ways to say the words to emphasize it. Also, where is Babylon? How many miles are *threescore and ten?* What is the unusual meaning of *candlelight?* (In this poem it's a way of saying *twilight,* the time for lighting candles.)

How Much Wood Would a Woodchuck Chuck

How much wood would a woodchuck chuck

If a woodchuck could chuck wood?

He would chuck as much wood as a woodchuck would chuck,

If a woodchuck could chuck wood.

SUGGESTION: Children need to know what woodchucks are so they can act like them as they try to recite this tricky tongue twister. This verse is just fun to say, and, like any tongue twister, children will want to try and say it faster and faster with each repetition. Having the printed version to read slowly as they learn the words will help.

fold
here

125

Humpty Dumpty

Humpty Dumpty sat on a wall,

Humpty Dumpty had a great fall;

All the king's horses and all the king's men

Couldn't put Humpty together again.

SUGGESTION: Children will have heard this traditional nursery rhyme before. You may want to use it as the basis for a discussion of many of the traditional Mother Goose rhymes they know, selecting their favorites or making comparisons between two or three selected rhymes. It is also a good example to revisit when discussing passives.

I Don't Suppose

I don't suppose

A lobster knows

The proper way

To blow his nose,

Or else perhaps

Beneath the seas

They have no need

to sniff and sneeze.

SUGGESTION: What a silly image: a lobster blowing his nose! Children will automatically add their own silly actions as they reread it several times. It is also a great verse to revisit when children are focusing on long *o* and long *e* sounds.

I Hear Thunder

I hear thunder, I hear thunder,

Hark don't you? Hark don't you?

Pitter patter raindrops, pitter patter raindrops,

I'm wet through, so are you!

I see blue skies, I see blue skies,

Way up high, way up high.

Hurry up the sunshine, hurry up the sunshine,

We'll soon dry, we'll soon dry.

SUGGESTION: Teach the children to sing the rhyme to the tune of "Are You Sleeping?" ("Frère Jacques"). There are many weather related verses in this volume. You might consider pairing this with some of them for a weather poetry session. A few examples are "Whether the Weather," "If All the Little Raindrops," "One Misty Moisty Morning," and "Jack Frost."

I Like Silver

I like silver.
I like brass.
I like looking
In the looking glass.

I like rubies.
I like pearls.
I like wearing
My hair in curls.

I like earrings.
I like clothes.
I like wearing
My hair in rows.

I like baseball.
I like bats.
I like wearing
Baseball hats.

SUGGESTION: Create some new verses with the same simple "I like…" rhythm and pattern.

I Live in the City

I live in the city, yes I do,
I live in the city, yes I do,
I live in the city, yes I do,
Made by human hands.

Black hands, white hands, tan and brown
All together built this town,
Black hands, white hands, tan and brown
All together make the wheels go 'round.

Black hands, brown hands, tan and white
Built the buildings tall and bright,
Black hands, brown hands, tan and white
Filled them all with shining light.

Black hands, white hands, brown and tan
Milled the flour and cleaned the pan,
Black hands, white hands, brown and tan
The working woman and the working man.

I live in the city, yes I do,
I live in the city, yes I do,
I live in the city, yes I do,
Made by human hands.

SUGGESTION: Children can talk about what is meant by the many different colors of hands in the poem. Three different groups can each learn one of the middle three verses as the colors are presented in varied order to create rhymes. Then they can recite their verse as appropriate.

I Never Saw a Purple Cow

by Gelette Burgess

I never saw a purple cow.

I never hope to see one.

But I can tell you anyhow

I'd rather see than be one.

SUGGESTION: Children will enjoy this nonsense verse and may make up and illustrate some of their own, for example, *I never saw a yellow goat. | I never hope to see one. | But I can tell you, and I quote, | I'd rather see than be one.* They might also like to make a class book with the poem on every page and a different color cow on each page.

I Raised a Great Hullabaloo

I raised a great hullabaloo

When I found a large mouse in my stew.

Said the waiter, "Don't shout

And wave it all about,

Or the rest will be wanting one, too."

SUGGESTION: This is a limerick that begs to be acted out. Children can take turns sitting in front of a bowl or paper cup and pulling out a large paper mouse. As a variation, they may invent other kinds of food and other unsavory items that might be found in them.

I Saw Esau

I saw Esau sawing wood,

And Esau saw I saw him.

Though Esau saw I saw him saw,

Still Esau went on sawing!

SUGGESTION: This is a tricky tongue twister. Have the children think about which syllables or words to stress and which to run together to convey the correct meaning. Have the children pause after the first line, read the second line quickly, pause after the third line, and read the last line quickly. A printed copy allows them to read and practice at their own pace.

fold
here

133

I Saw a Ship A-sailing

I saw a ship a-sailing,
A-sailing on the sea;
And, oh! it was all laden
With pretty things for thee!

There were candies in the cabin,
And apples in the hold.
The sails were made of silk,
And the masts were made of gold.

The four-and-twenty sailors
That stood between the decks,
Were four-and-twenty white mice,
With chains about their necks.

The captain was a duck
With a pack upon her back.
And when the ship began to move,
The captain said, "Quack! Quack!"

SUGGESTION: Children love reciting and illustrating this poem. They can make a poetry chart for each stanza, adding their own cutout drawings to the printed text. This is a good project for group work.

I Thought

I thought a thought.

But the thought I thought

Wasn't the thought I thought I thought.

If the thought I thought I thought,

Had been the thought I thought,

I wouldn't have thought so much.

SUGGESTION: Children will want to ponder the meaning of each line, noticing how *thought* can be a noun and a verb. Also, stringing *I thought* together adds to and changes the meaning. Children can actually add more lines to the poem, playing with words in the same way.

fold
here

135

I Went Downtown

I went downtown
To see Mrs. Brown.

She gave me a nickel
To buy a pickle.

The pickle was sour,
She gave me a flower.

The flower was dead,
She gave me a thread.

The thread was thin,
She gave me a pin.

The pin was sharp,
She gave me a harp.

And the harp began to sing—

Minnie and a minnie
And a ha ha ha!

SUGGESTION: This poem reinforces rhyming words. Children can predict each new item given by Mrs. Brown based on the word at the end of the preceding line, as well as create their own rhymes. Ask class members to read the first and last verses together, but divide up to read other verses.

I Went to the Pictures Tomorrow

I went to the pictures tomorrow,

I took a front seat at the back.

I fell from the pit to the gallery,

And broke a front bone in my back.

A lady she gave me some chocolate,

I ate it and gave it her back.

I phoned for a taxi and walked it,

And that's why I never came back.

SUGGESTION: This nonsense poem is full of contrasts. You might want to make a chart with children listing them.

fold
here

137

If All the Little Raindrops

If all the little raindrops
Were lemondrops and gumdrops
Oh, what a rain that would be!
Standing outside, with my mouth open wide
Ah, ah, ah, ah, ah, ah, ah, ah, ah, ah
If all the raindrops
Were lemondrops and gumdrops
Oh, what a rain that would be!

If all the little snowflakes
Were candy bars and milkshakes
Oh, what a snow that would be!
Standing outside, with my mouth open wide
Ah, ah, ah, ah, ah, ah, ah, ah, ah, ah
If all the snowflakes
Were candy bars and milkshakes
Oh, what a snow that would be!

If all the little sunbeams
Were bubblegum and ice cream
Oh, what a sun that would be!
Standing outside, with my mouth open wide
Ah, ah, ah, ah, ah, ah, ah, ah, ah, ah
If all the sunbeams
Were bubblegum and ice cream
Oh, what a sun that would be!

SUGGESTION: Children can pretend to be catching the sweets on their tongues as they say *ah*, or they can say *ah* with appreciation. They can substitute other favorite foods for the items in the poem by thinking of what would rhyme with *raindrops*, *snowflakes*, and *sunbeams*. Other weather words could be used as well.

If All the Seas Were One Sea

If all the seas were one sea,

What a great sea it would be!

And if all the trees were one tree,

What a great tree it would be!

And if all the axes were one axe,

What a great axe it would be!

And if all the men were one man,

What a great man he would be!

And if the great man took the great axe

And cut down the great tree

And let it fall into the great sea,

What a great splish-splash that would be!

SUGGESTION: To perform the poem, one group can read the *if* lines; the other, the lines beginning with *What*. Then the whole class reads the last two lines. Finger puppets could be used to help with comprehension. This poem is useful for studying the formation of plurals.

fold
here

139

If All the World Were Apple Pie

If all the world were apple pie,

And all the sea were ink,

If all the trees

Were bread and cheese,

What should we have to drink?

SUGGESTION: This poem juxtaposes some strange ideas that children will like to try to imagine. They can talk about how imagination is used to make the poem interesting and think of some fantastic ideas of their own.

If Wishes Were Horses

If wishes were horses,

Beggars would ride;

If turnips were watches,

I would wear one by my side.

SUGGESTION: Children may find it intriguing to discuss the meaning of the two expressions. Invite your class to create some new *If* _____ *were* _____ verses.

fold
here

141

If You Ever

If you ever, ever, ever

Meet a grizzly bear,

You will never, never, never

Meet another grizzly bear.

If you ever, ever, ever,

If you ever meet a whale,

You must never, never, never,

You must never touch its tail,

For if you ever, ever, ever,

If you ever touch its tail,

You will never, never, never,

Meet another whale.

SUGGESTION: Your class will enjoy the joke about why they would *never, never, never* / *Meet another grizzly bear.* Create your own *If you ever,* / *You will never* verses together using the same structure: *If you ever, ever, ever* _____ / *You will never, never, never* _____. Patterns like this help children understand language and give them predictable structures to build on.

If You Notice

If you noticed this notice,

You will notice

That this notice

Is not worth noticing.

SUGGESTION: This whimsical jingle is fun to post in the classroom. Children can talk about what makes it humorous. Also, draw attention to the different uses of *notice* (as a verb, noun, and gerund).

If You're Happy and You Know It

If you're happy and you know it,

Clap your hands.

If you're happy and you know it,

Clap your hands.

If you're happy and you know it,

Then your face will surely show it.

If you're happy and you know it,

Clap your hands.

ACTIONS:
If you're happy and you know it,
Clap your hands. [*clap, clap*]
If you're happy and you know it,
Clap your hands. [*clap, clap*]
If you're happy and you know it,
Then your face will surely show it. [*smile*]
If you're happy and you know it,
Clap your hands. [*clap, clap*]

SUGGESTION: Perform this poem as an action rhyme. Have children switch sides and say the poem a second time. Add actions such as *stomp your feet* or *stand and cheer*. Children's familiarity with this makes it a great poem to revisit when working with *are* contractions.

I'm a Frozen Icicle

I'm a frozen icicle

Hanging by your door.

When it's cold outside,

I grow even more.

When it's warm outside,

You'll find me on the floor!

SUGGESTION: Children who have never seen *icicles* will find them fascinating. Teach the poem and talk about icicles. Children can talk about the effects of cold and warmth on water.

In the Morning

This is the way

We brush our teeth

Brush our teeth

Brush our teeth.

This is the way

We brush our teeth

So early in the morning.

SUGGESTION: Most children will know this simple verse sung to the tune of "The Mulberry Bush." They love to create new verses about activities they do throughout the day: *go to school, ride the bus, eat our lunch,* etc. For children this age—the sillier, the better. That's why it is a good song to revisit when working with homonyms. The poem has several examples (*way, our, so, in*), and children can use their lists of homonyms to extend this song. This is the way we *ate* the *eight;* This is how we *know* it's *no.*

Intery, Mintery, Cutery, Corn

Intery, mintery, cutery, corn,

Apple seed and apple thorn;

Wire, briar, limber lock,

Three geese in a flock.

One flew east,

And one flew west,

And one flew over the cuckoo's nest.

SUGGESTION: Have all the children chant the first four lines; assign "soloists" for the final three lines.

fold
here

147

The Itsy, Bitsy Spider

The itsy, bitsy spider

Climbed up the waterspout.

Down came the rain

And washed the spider out.

Out came the sun

And dried up all the rain.

And the itsy, bitsy spider

Climbed up the spout again.

SUGGESTION: This old favorite is so familiar to children that revisiting it when they are using letter clusters to solve words is a natural.

I've Been Working on the Railroad

I've been working on the railroad,
All the live long day,
I've been working on the railroad,
Just to pass the time away.
Don't you hear the whistle blowing?
Rise up so early in the morn.
Don't you hear the captain shouting,
Dinah, blow your horn?

Dinah, won't you blow,
Dinah, won't you blow,
Dinah, won't you blow your horn?
Dinah, won't you blow,
Dinah, won't you blow,
Dinah, won't you blow your horn?

Someone's in the kitchen with Dinah,
Someone's in the kitchen, I know,
Someone's in the kitchen with Dinah
Strumming on the old banjo.

Fee, fie, fiddle-e-i-o
Fee, fie, fiddle-e-i-o-o-o-o.
Fee, fie, fiddle-e-i-o,
Strumming on the old banjo.

SUGGESTION: This is an old folk song. Children can accompany the refrain with simple rhythm instruments.

fold
here

149

Jack Frost

Jack Frost bites your nose.

He chills your cheeks and freezes your toes.

He comes every year when winter is here

And stays until spring is near.

SUGGESTION: Teach children the meaning of personification: Jack Frost is the personification of frost or very wintry weather. Children may find it fun to draw and share their own versions of Jack Frost.

Jack Sprat

Jack Sprat could eat no fat,

His wife could eat no lean.

And so between them both, you see,

They licked the platter clean.

Lily only goes out in the day,

Her brother goes only at night.

And because they never see each other,

They never get into a fight.

SUGGESTION: All your children will know this favorite. Have children read both verses and point out the antonyms. Then challenge them to use their antonym lists and the poem as a model to create new verses.

Jack-a-Nory

I'll tell you a story

About Jack-a-Nory,

And now my story's begun;

I'll tell you another

About his brother,

And now my story is done!

SUGGESTION: Have groups of children read alternate lines and then all read the final line together. Discuss what makes this humorous and the idea of "story."

Jack-in-the-box

Jack-in-the-box,

All shut up tight,

Not a breath of air,

Not a ray of light.

You must be so tired,

Waiting all night,

We'd open your lid,

But you'd give us a fright.

SUGGESTION: Children may know several variations of this old favorite. This particular version provides the perfect introduction to the common spelling pattern -ight. Pair it with "Star Light, Star Bright" and you've covered most of words with
that pattern in children's vocabularies.

Jelly on the Plate

Jelly on the plate.
Jelly on the plate.
Wibble, wobble,
Wibble, wobble,
Jelly on the plate.

Pudding in the pan.
Pudding in the pan.
Ooey, gooey,
Ooey, gooey,
Pudding in the pan.

Soup in the pot.
Soup in the pot.
Bubble, bubble,
Bubble, bubble,
Soup in the pot.

Snowflakes on my nose.
Snowflakes on my nose.
Sniffle, snuffle,
Sniffle, snuffle,
Snowflakes on my nose.

continued

SUGGESTION: The nonsense words in this classic are fun for children to pantomime as they recite the words. They will love making up new verses once they get the hang of the poem's structure.

Raindrops in my shoes.
Raindrops in my shoes.
Sloshy, slushy,
Sloshy, slushy,
Raindrops in my shoes.

Cookies on the plate.
Cookies on the plate.
Gobble, gobble,
Gobble, gobble,
Cookies on the plate.

Jingle Jangle

Jingle jangle

Silver bangle

You look cute

From every angle.

SUGGESTION: Children can talk about who is being addressed in this poem. They can take it literally—that it is a bangle bracelet—or figuratively—that it is a person or animal.

John Jacob Jingleheimer Schmidt

John Jacob Jingleheimer Schmidt

His name is my name, too!

Whenever we go out,

The people always shout

There goes John Jacob Jingleheimer Schmidt!

Da da da da da da da.

SUGGESTION: This is an old camp song with a surprise ending. Children can sing the verse several times, each time with a softer voice. They shout *Da da da da da da da* each time they reach the last line. For the music, try a CD, such as *Drew's Famous Kids Camp Songs*, sung by a variety of artists.

fold here

157

Kitten Is Hiding

A kitten is hiding under a chair.

I looked and I looked for her everywhere,

Under the table and under the bed.

I looked in the corner, and when I said,

"Come, kitty, come, kitty, here's milk for you,"

Kitty came running, calling, "Mew, mew, mew."

SUGGESTION: Children might be familiar with this poem. If so, they can act it out as they recite it. Because all the words
are probably within your children's oral-language vocabulary, it is a good poem to revisit when using word-solving actions
to divide words into syllables.

Knock, Knock

"Knock, knock"

"Who's there?"

"Lettuce."

"Lettuce who?"

"Lettuce in, it's cold out here."

SUGGESTION: Children enjoy the *knock knock* genre of jokes and will say them over and over. Use this poem to illustrate how a *knock knock* joke plays on words and how they sound. Children can make up their own jokes or ask family members to tell more of them.

A Lady Went A-marketing

A lady went a-marketing—

She bought a little fish;

She put it in a crystal bowl

Upon a golden dish.

An hour she sat in wonderment

And watched its silver gleam,

And then she gently took it up

And slipped it in a stream.

SUGGESTION: This poem tells a story about buying something pretty to look at in captivity but then setting it free. Children can tell the story in prose to contrast the form with the poem, and they may discuss reasons why the lady put the fish in a stream. You might also lead the discussion to decisions about what kind of creatures might be let free (captured turtles, spiders, etc.) and what kind should not be (caged birds that could not survive in the wild).

The Land of Counterpane

by Robert Louis Stevenson

When I was sick and lay a-bed,

I had two pillows at my head,

And all my toys beside me lay

To keep me happy all the day.

And sometimes for an hour or so

I watched my leaden soldiers go,

With different uniforms and drills,

Among the bed-clothes, through the hills.

And sometimes sent my ships in fleets

All up and down among the sheets;

Or brought my trees and houses out,

And planted cities all about.

I was the giant great and still

That sits upon the pillow-hill,

And sees before him dale and plain,

The pleasant land of counterpane.

SUGGESTION: Have children listen to the poem several times as you read it aloud. They can then talk about the meaning of the poem (the writer comparing himself to a giant because he is playing with miniature people and ships). They may discuss their own experiences playing with cars or talk about what they do when they are sick and have to stay in bed.

Little Arabella Miller

Little Arabella Miller

Had a fuzzy caterpillar.

First it crawled upon her mother,

Then upon her baby brother.

They said, "Arabella Miller,

Put away that caterpillar!"

Little Arabella Miller

Had a great big green snake.

First it crawled upon her mother,

Then upon her baby brother.

They said, "Arabella Miller,

Put away that great big green snake!"

SUGGESTION: The repetition of *er* endings makes this poem enjoyable, and the *ar* sounds the same in *caterpillar.* Have children say it with rhythm. They can think of innovations. After they know the poem, you can call attention to word endings.

Little Robin Redbreast

Little Robin Redbreast

Sat upon a rail;

Niddle, noddle went his head,

Wiggle, waggle went his tail.

Little Robin Redbreast

Sat upon a hurdle,

With a pair of speckled legs,

And a green girdle.

SUGGESTION: Children may recite the poem as well as perform it as a finger play. The nonsense words *niddle, noddle* add interest. Ask the group to invent other nonsense words that fit the actions of the verse. It will be helpful for English-language learners to see a photo of a robin and other birds.

fold
here

163

The Littlest Worm

The littlest worm   (The littlest worm)
You ever saw   (You ever saw)
Got stuck inside   (Got stuck inside)
My soda straw.   (My soda straw.)

The littlest worm you ever saw
Got stuck inside my soda straw.

He said to me   (He said to me)
"Don't take a sip   ("Don't take a sip)
Cause if you do   (Cause if you do)
You'll get real sick."   (You'll get real sick.")

He said to me "Don't take a sip,
Cause if you do you'll get real sick."

I took a sip   (I took a sip)
And he went down   (And he went down)
Right through my pipe   (Right through my pipe)
He must have drowned.   (He must have drowned.)

I took a sip and he went down
Right through my pipe he must have drowned.

continued

SUGGESTION: This poem is intended to be performed in "echo" fashion, with one part of the group saying the line and another repeating it immediately. Do this for the first four lines, and then have everyone say lines 6 and 7 together, repeating the process throughout the poem. Sing to the tune of "The Prettiest Girl I Ever Saw Was Sipping Cider Through a Straw."

He was my pal   (He was my pal)
He was my friend   (He was my friend)
There is no more   (There is no more)
This is the end.   (This is the end.)

He was my pal he was my friend
There is no more this is the end.

Now don't you fret   (Now don't you fret)
Now don't you fear   (Now don't you fear)
That little worm   (That little worm)
Had scuba gear.   (Had scuba gear.)

Now don't you fret now don't you fear
That little worm had scuba gear.

Make New Friends

Make new friends,

But keep the old.

One is silver,

And the other's gold.

SUGGESTION: What kinds of images do the words *gold* and *silver* bring to mind? Let children discuss why the poet uses these words to tell us about friendship.

Mary Wore Her Red Dress

Mary wore her red dress, red dress, red dress.
Mary wore her red dress
All day long.

Mary wore her red hat, red hat, red hat.
Mary wore her red hat
All day long.

Mary wore her red shoes, red shoes, red shoes.
Mary wore her red shoes
All day long.

Mary wore her red gloves, red gloves, red gloves.
Mary wore her red gloves
All day long.

Mary was a red bird, red bird, red bird.
Mary was a red bird
All day long!

SUGGESTION: This is an old Texas folk song. Pair it with the story of Kate Bear's birthday party in Merle Peek's picture book *Mary Wore Her Red Dress and Henry Wore His Green Sneakers*. Eliminate the last verse and make it a poem about different children wearing different-color clothes. Children enjoy substituting their own names and color choices.

Michael Finnegan

There was an old man named Michael Finnegan.
He had whiskers on his chinnegan.
They fell out and then grew in again.
Poor old Michael Finnegan,
Begin again.

There was an old man named Michael Finnegan.
He went fishing with a pin again.
Caught a fish and dropped it in again.
Poor old Michael Finnegan,
Begin again.

There was an old man named Michael Finnegan.
He grew fat and then grew thin again.
Then he died and had to begin again.
Poor old Michael Finnegan,
Begin again.

SUGGESTION: Help children see how repeating patterns (using one or more words said together quickly) are used to create rhymes and make a humorous poem. They will enjoy reciting the poem, especially the part that says *Begin again*, which suddenly switches from *Michael Finnegan* to instructing the readers/performers.

Milkman, Milkman

Milkman, milkman,

Where have you been?

Buttermilk Channel, up to my chin.

I spilled my milk,

And I spoiled my clothes

And I got a long icicle

Hung from my nose.

SUGGESTION: Have some children read the initial two-line question and the rest of the children read the response. This simple verse is a good one to use when children are identifying long and short vowel sounds in words. Or return to it when looking for examples of adding *ed* to form past tense.

fold
here

169

Miss Mary Mack

Miss Mary Mack, Mack, Mack
All dressed in black, black, black
With silver buttons, buttons, buttons
All down her back, back, back.
She asked her mother, mother, mother
For fifteen cents, cents, cents
To see the elephants, elephants, elephants
Jump the fence, fence, fence.
They jumped so high, high, high
They touched the sky, sky, sky,
And they didn't come down, down, down
Till the fourth of July, ly, ly.

SUGGESTION: Hand-clapping games are good practice for coordination and rhythm. Have the children play a clapping game with a partner. They clap their partner's palms face front, then their own hands, and then their partners palms again on the first set of repeated words. Then they cross their arms when they clap their partner's palms on the next three repeated words. They continue this alternation and clap thighs for the last repeat—*down, down, down*. Use with the rollicking picture book *Miss Mary Mack* by Mary Ann Hoberman.

Miss Polly Had a Dolly

Miss Polly had a dolly
Who was sick, sick, sick,
So she sent for the doctor
To be quick, quick, quick.

The doctor came
With his bag and hat,
And he knocked at the door
With a rat-a-tat-tat.

He looked at the dolly
And he shook his head,
And he said, "Miss Polly,
Put her straight to bed."

He wrote out a paper
For a pill, pill, pill,
"That'll make her better,
Yes it will, will, will!"

Mr. Crocodile

Three little monkeys swinging from a tree,

Teasing Mr. Crocodile, "You can't catch me!"

Along came Mr. Crocodile, quiet as can be . . . SNAP!

Two little monkeys swinging from a tree,

Teasing Mr. Crocodile, "You can't catch me!"

Along came Mr. Crocodile, quiet as can be . . . SNAP!

One little monkey swinging from a tree,

Teasing Mr. Crocodile, "You can't catch me!"

Along came Mr. Crocodile, quiet as can be . . . SNAP!

"MISSED ME!"

SUGGESTION: Have the children clap along at each *SNAP* and all shout, *MISSED ME!*

Mr. Nobody

I know a funny little man,
As quiet as a mouse,
Who does the mischief that is done
In everybody's house!

There's no one ever sees his face,
And yet we all agree
That every plate we break was cracked
By Mr. Nobody.

It's he who always tears our books,
Who leaves the door ajar.
He pulls the buttons from our shirts,
And scatters pins afar.

He puts damp wood upon the fire,
That kettles cannot boil;
His are the feet that bring in mud
And all the carpets soil.

The finger marks upon the door
By none of us are made;
We never leave the blinds unclosed,
To let the curtains fade.

The ink we never spill; the boots
That lying 'round you see
Are not our boots—they all belong
To Mr. Nobody.

SUGGESTION: Make a list together of all the things "Mr. Nobody" could be responsible for. Scribe for the children or let them share the pen. (The list will be fun to illustrate.) Read back the list for a great shared reading experience.

Monday's Child

Monday's child is fair of face,

Tuesday's child is full of grace,

Wednesday's child is full of woe,

Thursday's child has far to go,

Friday's child is loving and giving,

Saturday's child works hard for a living,

But the child born on Sunday

Is bonny and blithe and good and gay.

SUGGESTION: This is an old rhyme about the days of the week. Ask your students to find out on which day they were born. Children born on the same day of the week can then work together to create a new rhyme for *Monday's child*, *Tuesday's child,* and so on.

The Months of the Year

January brings the snow,
Makes our feet and fingers glow.

February brings the rain,
Thaws the frozen lake again.

March brings breezes loud and shrill,
Stirs the dancing daffodil.

April brings the primrose sweet,
Scatters daisies at our feet.

May brings flocks of pretty lambs,
Skipping by their fleecy dams.

June brings tulips, lilies, roses,
Fills the children's hands with posies.

continued

SUGGESTION: Children may pair off to read or recite these verses, alternating each month. As an alternative, partners could be assigned a month and asked to act out (or create drawings to hold up) as they perform their lines in unison. The partners could present in calendar order. This is also a good poem to revisit for vowel combinations (*ai, ay, ea, ee, ow*) and again for recognizing syllables.

Hot July brings cooling showers,
Apricots, and gillyflowers.

August brings the sheaves of corn,
Then the harvest home is borne.

Clear September brings blue skies,
Goldenrod, and apple pies.

Fresh October brings the pheasant,
Then to gather nuts is pleasant.

Dull November brings the blast,
Makes the leaves go whirling fast.

Chill December brings the sleet,
Blazing fire, and holiday treat.

The Moon

by Robert Louis Stevenson

The moon has a face like the clock in the hall;

She shines on thieves on the garden wall,

On streets and fields and harbor quays,

And birdies asleep in the forks of the trees.

The squalling cat and the squeaking mouse,

The howling dog by the door of the house,

The bat that lies in bed at noon,

All love to be out by the light of the moon.

But all of the things that belong to the day

Cuddle to sleep to be out of her way;

And flowers and children close their eyes

Till up in the morning the sun shall rise.

SUGGESTION: A few words, especially *harbor quays*, may need explaining. (The rhyme will help children with the pronunciation of the word *quays*. It rhymes with *trees*.) Teach children about similes—comparisons of two unlike things, especially in phrases containing the words *like* or *as*. Invite children to create their own similes about the moon: *The moon has a face like* _____ .

Moses Supposes

Moses supposes his toeses are roses,

But Moses supposes erroneously;

For nobody's toeses are posies of roses,

As Moses supposes his toeses to be.

SUGGESTION: Help children hear the playful language sounds as they recite and read the verse. When they are familiar with the language, they may read it more quickly. A poetry chart of this poem could be posted as a reference for long *o* sounds: *Moses, supposes, toeses, roses,* and so forth.

A Mouse in Her Room

A mouse in her room woke Miss Dowd,

Who was frightened and screamed very loud.

Then a happy thought hit her—

To scare off the critter

She sat up in her bed and meowed.

SUGGESTION: Invite children to talk about why what Miss Dowd did was so clever. They'll need to think from the mouse's perspective! What if Miss Dowd had an elephant in her room? Or a bug?

fold here

179

The Mulberry Bush

Here we go 'round the mulberry bush,

The mulberry bush, the mulberry bush.

Here we go 'round the mulberry bush,

So early in the morning.

ADDITIONAL VERSES:

This is the way we wash our clothes,
Wash our clothes, wash our clothes.
This is the way we wash our clothes,
So early Monday morning.

This is the way we iron our clothes,
Iron our clothes, iron our clothes.
This is the way we iron our clothes,
So early Tuesday morning.

This is the way we mend our clothes,
Mend our clothes, mend our clothes.
This is the way we mend our clothes,
So early Wednesday morning.

This is the way we scrub the floor,
Scrub the floor, scrub the floor.
This is the way we scrub the floor,
So early Thursday morning.

This is the way we sweep the house,
Sweep the house, sweep the house.
This is the way we sweep the house,
So early Friday morning.

This is the way we bake our bread,
Bake our bread, bake our bread.
This is the way we bake our bread,
So early Saturday morning.

This is the way we walk the dog,
Walk the dog, walk the dog.
This is the way we walk the dog,
So early Sunday morning.

fold
here

SUGGESTION: Children enjoy singing the song and pantomiming the actions. They can invent their own updated verses: *This is the way we ride our bikes, This is the way we play in the park*, and so on.

My Father Is Extremely Tall

My father is extremely tall

When he stands upright like a wall—

But I am very short and small.

Yet I am growing, so they say,

A little taller every day.

SUGGESTION: Children can recite the poem as they "act out" the idea of being *tall* and *small*. Help them see that all measurements are relative: to a mouse, we are tall, yet we are very small compared with an elephant. Children could draw themselves next to two different animals and label themselves as either "small" or "tall" in each comparative drawing.

fold
here

181

My Love for You

I know you little,

I love you lots;

My love for you

Would fill ten pots,

Fifteen buckets,

Sixteen cans,

Three teacups,

And four dishpans.

SUGGESTION: After reading this verse several times (and perhaps using it in a pocket chart), ask children to substitute other number words in this poem.

My Old Hen

I went down to my garden patch

To see if my old hen had hatched.

She'd hatched out her chickens and the peas were green.

She sat there a-peckin' on a tambourine.

SUGGESTION: Children may enjoy talking about and drawing the images in this poem. They could also shake a tambourine as they say the poem. They may discuss that the poem's images are realistic until the last line where the poem becomes fanciful.

fold
here

183

My Shadow

by Robert Louis Stevenson

I have a little shadow that goes in and out with me,

And what can be the use of him is more than I can see.

He is very, very like me from the heels up to the head:

And I see him jump before me when I jump into my bed.

The funniest thing about him is the way he likes to grow:

Not at all like proper children, which is always very slow.

For he sometimes shoots up taller like an india-rubber ball,

And he sometimes gets so little that there's none of him at all.

SUGGESTION: Have the children swing back and forth at the beginning of the first verse, stretch up at the beginning of
the second verse, and curl up at the end. After they learn this poem, children may enjoy creating shadow art. Have them
cut out their own image from a drawing placed over a piece of black paper. This will produce two cutout images; the
drawing and a black shadow. Attaching both cutouts to paper, with feet touching, creates a real shadow picture.

Nest Eggs

by Robert Louis Stevenson

Here in the fork

The brown nest is seated;

Four little blue eggs

The mother keeps heated.

SUGGESTION: Children may need a little help puzzling out this poem. Have them brainstorm the meaning of *fork* in this context, and discuss how and why the mother bird heats the eggs. Pair this playful poem with a nonfiction book about birds or nests, such as *About Birds*, by Cathryn Sill.

fold here

185

New Shoes

My shoes are new and squeaky shoes,

They're shiny, creaky shoes,

I wish I had my leaky shoes

That my mother threw away.

I liked my old brown leaky shoes,

Much better than these creaky shoes,

These shiny, creaky, squeaky shoes

I've got to wear today.

SUGGESTION: Children will be able to relate to the idea that shoes you have worn a long time might be more comfortable than new shoes, although they may really enjoy wearing the new ones. Some volunteers can illustrate this poem with pictures of old and new shoes.

New Sights

I like to see a thing I know

Has not been seen before,

That's why I cut my apple through

To look into the core.

It's nice to think, though many an eye

Has seen the ruddy skin,

Mine is the very first to spy

The five brown pips within.

SUGGESTION: This poem is about seeing something familiar with new eyes. Children may find it a unique idea to know that if they are looking at the inside of an apple or orange, they are probably the first to see it. Help them understand that *pips* are seeds.

fold
here

187

Night

The sun descending in the west

The evening star does shine;

The birds are silent in their nest,

And I must seek for mine.

The moon like a flower

In heaven's high bower,

With silent delight

Sits and smiles on the night.

SUGGESTION: Children will enjoy talking about the comparisons in this poem—a nest with your own bed, the moon and a flower, heaven and a garden. They can also notice the parts of the poem that make the moon seem like a person—to be alive.

A Nonsense Alphabet

by Edward Lear

A was once an apple pie,
Pidy
Widy
Tidy
Pidy
Nice Insidy
Apple Pie!

B was once a little bear,
Beary
Wary
Hairy
Beary
Taky Cary
Little Bear!

C was once a little cake,
Caky
Baky
Maky
Caky
Taky Caky,
Little Cake!

D was once a little doll,
Dolly
Molly
Polly
Dolly
Nursey Dolly
Little Doll!

E was once a little eel,
Eely
Weely
Peely
Eely
Twirly Tweely
Little Eel!

F was once a little fish,
Fishy
Wishy
Squishy
Fishy
In a Dishy
Little Fish!

continued

SUGGESTION: This sophisticated alphabet poem could be the basis of personal alphabet books for children, which they can illustrate. Since they will already know the alphabet, help them see how word play forms the basis of the book and how to use the alphabet as an organizing tool. They can perform the poem with each child reading a verse.

G was once a little goose,
Goosey
Moosey
Boosey
Goosey
Waddly Woosey
Little Goose!

H was once a little hen,
Henny
Chenny
Tenny
Henny
Eggsy Any
Little Hen?

I was once a bottle of ink,
Inky
Dinky
Thinky
Inky
Blacky Minky
Bottle of Ink!

J was once a jar of jam,
Jammy
Mammy
Clammy
Jammy
Sweety Swammy
Jar of Jam!

K was once a little kite,
Kity
Whity
Flighty
Kity
Out of Sighty
Little Kite!

L was once a little lark,
Larky
Marky
Harky
Larky
In the Parky
Little Lark!

continued

M was once a little mouse,
Mousey
Bousey
Sousey
Mousey
In the Housey
Little Mouse!

N was once a little needle,
Needly
Tweedly
Threedly
Needly
Wisky Wheedly
Little Needle!

O was once a little owl,
Owly
Prowly
Howly
Owly
Browny Fowly
Little Owl!

P was once a little pump,
Pumpy
Slumpy
Flumpy
Pumpy
Dumpy Thumpy
Little Pump!

Q was once a little quail,
Quaily
Faily
Daily
Quaily
Stumpy Taily
Little Quail!

R was once a little rose,
Rosy
Posy
Nosy
Rosy
Blows-y Grows-y
Little Rose!

continued

S was once a little shrimp,
Shrimpy
Nimpy
Flimpy
Shrimpy
Jumpy Jimpy
Little Shrimp!

T was once a little thrush,
Thrushy
Hushy
Bushy
Thrushy
Flitty Flushy
Little Thrush!

U was once a little urn,
Urny
Burny
Turny
Urny
Bubbly Burny
Little Urn!

V was once a little vine,
Viny
Winy
Twiny
Viny
Twisty Twiny
Little Vine!

W was once a mighty whale,
Whaly
Scaly
Shaly
Whaly
Tumbly Taily
Mighty Whale!

X was once a great king Xerxes,
Xerxy
Perxy
Turxy
Xerxy
Linxy Lurxy
Great King Xerxes!

Y was once a little yew,
Yewdy
Fewdy
Crudy
Yewdy
Growdy Grewdy,
Little Yew!

Z was once a piece of zinc,
Zinky
Winky
Blinky
Zinky
Tinky Minky
Piece of Zinc!

The North Wind Doth Blow

The north wind doth blow,

And we shall have snow,

And what will the robin do then, poor thing?

He'll sit in the barn,

And keep himself warm,

And hide his head under his wing, poor thing!

SUGGESTION: Mood is the important thing to aim for with this poem. Teach children to recite the words slowly, with their voices suggesting cold and shivery weather. For a finale, they may tuck their heads under their *wings*. Suggest that *doth* is an old way of saying *does*.

fold
here

193

Not a Word

They walked the lane together,

The sky was dotted with stars,

They reached the rails together,

He lifted up the bars.

She neither smiled nor thanked him,

Because she knew not how,

For he was only the farmer's boy

And she was the jersey cow!

SUGGESTION: Cover the last two lines of the poem and have the children predict how it will end. Then uncover the surprise!

Now We Are Gathering Nuts in May

Now we are gathering nuts in May,
Nuts in May, nuts in May,
Now we are gathering nuts in May
Out on a frosty morning.

Who will come over for nuts in May,
Nuts in May, nuts in May,
Who will come over for nuts in May
Out on a frosty morning?

Sue will come over for nuts in May,
Nuts in May, nuts in May,
Sue will come over for nuts in May
Out on a frosty morning.

Who will come over to fetch her away,
Fetch her away, fetch her away,
Who will come over to fetch her away
Out on a frosty morning?

Jack will come over to fetch her away,
Fetch her away, fetch her away,
Jack will come over to fetch her away
Out on a frosty morning.

SUGGESTION: Sing to the tune of "The Mulberry Bush."

Oh, How Lovely Is the Evening

Oh, how lovely is the evening,

Is the evening,

When the bells are sweetly ringing,

Sweetly ringing,

Ding, dong, ding, dong, ding, dong.

SUGGESTION: Once children know this poem they may use the pattern to create new verses: *Oh, how* _____ *is the* _____. (*Oh, how tricky is our math time* / *Oh, how funny is the classroom,* and so on.) You can also use this song to teach children how to sing a "round."

Oh, Susanna!

I come from Alabama
With my banjo on my knee;
I'm going to Lousiana,
My true love for to see.
It rained all night the day I left,
The weather it was dry;
The sun so hot I froze to death,
Susanna, don't you cry.

Oh, Susanna! Oh, don't you cry for me,
I come from Alabama with my banjo on my knee.

I had a dream the other night
When everything was still;
I thought I saw Susanna come
A-walking down the hill.
The red, red rose was in her hand,
The tear was in her eye;
I said, "I come from Alabam',
Susanna, don't you cry."

Oh, Susanna! Oh, don't you cry for me,
I come from Alabama with my banjo on my knee.

SUGGESTION: Teach children this old folk song. The vocabulary makes it a good verse to review, recognizing (or clapping) syllables in two-, three-, four-, and even five-syllable words.

Old King Cole

Old King Cole was a merry old soul,
And a merry old soul was he.
He called for his pipe
And he called for his bowl,
And he called for his fiddlers three.

Each fiddler he had a fiddle,
And the fiddles went tweedle-dee.
Oh, there's none so rare as can compare
As King Cole and his fiddlers three.

ADDITIONAL VERSES:

Then he called for his fifers two,
And they puffed and they blew tootle-too.
And King Cole laughed as his glass he quaffed,
And his fifers puffed tootle-too.

Then he called for his drummer boy,
The army's pride and joy.
And the thuds rang out with a loud bang, bang,
The noise of the noisiest toy.

Then he called for his trumpeters four,
Who stood at his own palace door.
And they played trang-a-tang
Whilst the drummer went bang,
And King Cole he called for more.

He called for a man to conduct,
Who into his bed had been tucked,
And he had to get up without bite or sup,
And waggle his stick and conduct.

Old King Cole laughed with glee,
Such rare antics to see.
There never was a man in merry England
Who was half as merry as he.

SUGGESTION: Children may be familiar with the first verse of this traditional rhyme but not the rest of the story. This rhyme-song has a great deal of rich language, with some vocabulary words that the children have never heard before (*quaffed, thuds, antics*) and complex language structure. Try making a strip mural with illustrations for each of the seven stanzas.

The Old Man and the Cow

by Edward Lear

There was an old man who said, "How

Shall I flee from this horrible cow?

I will sit on this stile,

And continue to smile,

Which may soften the heart of that cow."

SUGGESTION: Edward Lear is the master of the limerick, which children enjoy for rhyme and rhythm. Use this poem to help them study limericks (number of lines, which lines rhyme, content) and talk about what makes them funny. Help the children notice the rhyming pattern by having them whisper or shout the rhyming words.

fold here

199

Old Mother Hubbard

Old Mother Hubbard went to the cupboard

To give her poor dog a bone.

But when she got there, the cupboard was bare,

And so the poor dog had none.

She went to the hatter's to buy him a hat.

When she came back he was feeding the cat.

She went to the barber's to buy him a wig.

When she came back he was dancing a jig.

She went to the tailor's to buy him a coat.

When she came back he was riding a goat.

She went to the cobbler's to buy him some shoes.

When she came back he was reading the news.

SUGGESTION: This is a great story poem about a dog whose owner, Mother Hubbard, goes out to buy him things. Create new verses with the same pattern. For example: *She went to the cleaner's to get him some clothes. | When she came back he was licking his toes.* This is also a good poem to revisit when discussing possessives.

Once I Saw a Bunny

Once I saw a bunny

And a green cabbage head.

"I think I'll have some cabbage,"

The little bunny said.

So he nibbled and he nibbled.

And he pricked his ears to say,

"Now I think it's time

I should be hopping on my way."

SUGGESTION: Some children may have bunnies for pets and know a lot about them. Note that this poem provides several examples of words with double consonants. Plan to revisit it when covering that during the year.

fold
here

201

Once I Saw a Little Bird

Once I saw a little bird

Come hop, hop, hop.

And I cried, "Little bird,

Will you stop, stop, stop?"

I was going to the window

To say, "How do you do?"

When he shook his little tail,

And away he flew.

SUGGESTION: Children can discuss how the poem shows the behavior of birds. The rhythm of the first part of the poem is very much like a bird hopping. Children may be able to observe birds on the playground or at home. This poem is a good one to post at a window.

One Bottle of Pop

One bottle of pop in the yard
Two bottles
Three bottles
Four bottles of pop in the yard
Five bottles
Six bottles
Seven bottles of pop in the yard
POP!

Don't throw your junk in my backyard
My backyard
My backyard
Don't throw your junk in my backyard
My backyard's full of POP!

Fish and chips and vinegar
Vinegar
Vinegar
Fish and chips and vinegar
Soda, soda, soda, POP!

SUGGESTION: The primary characteristic of this poem is the rhythm. Have children try out different ways of saying the poem and use rhythm sticks to emphasize the cadences they choose. Make the word *pop* sound like a pop or use sound effects instead of saying the word.

One Misty, Moisty Morning

One misty, moisty morning,

When cloudy was the weather,

There I met an old man

Clothed all in leather.

He began to compliment

And I began to grin,

"How-do-you-do,"

And "How-do-you-do,"

And "How-do-you-do," again.

SUGGESTION: All the *s*'s in this poem set a foggy, moist mood. Children may take turns acting the poem out—one can be the child, one the old man. Or groups of children may recite the different parts of the poem as the child and old man take off invisible hats, bow, and say *How-do-you-do?* Be sure to revisit this poem when making connections between words that start the same (*misty, moisty, morning, met, man; cloudy, clothed,* etc.).

One Old Oxford Ox

One old Oxford ox opening oysters.

Two toads totally tired trying to trot to Tisbury.

Three thick thumping tigers taking toast for tea.

Four finicky fishermen fishing for funny fish.

Five frippery Frenchmen foolishly fishing for frogs.

Six sportsmen shooting snipe.

Seven Severn salmon swallowing shrimp.

Eight eminent Englishmen eagerly examining England.

Nine nibbling noblemen nibbling nectarines.

Ten tinkering tinkers tinkering ten tin tinderboxes.

Eleven elephants elegantly equipped.

Twelve typographical topographers typically translating types.

One, Two, Buckle My Shoe

One, two,

Buckle my shoe.

Three, four,

Knock at the door.

Five, six,

Pick up sticks.

Seven, eight,

Lay them straight.

Nine, ten,

A big fat hen.

SUGGESTION: Chances are, most children will have known this rhyme since kindergarten. If so, children can enjoy creating innovations, for example: *One, two, / go to the zoo. / Three, four, / Scrub the floor,* etc. They may work as partners.

The Orchestra

Oh! We can play on the big bass drum,

And this is the way we do it;

Rub-a-dub, boom, goes the big bass drum,

And this is the way we do it.

Oh! We can play on the violin,

And this is the way we do it;

Zum, zum, zin, says the violin,

Rub-a-dub, boom, goes the big bass drum,

And this is the way we do it.

Oh! We can play on the little flute,

And this is the way we do it;

Tootle, toot, toot, says the little flute,

Zum, zum, zin, goes the violin,

Rub-a-dub, boom, goes the big bass drum,

And this is the way we do it.

SUGGESTION: In this cumulative verse, each instrument is added to the previous one to build an orchestra. To help them recall the order, you can write the words for each instrument noise on a separate paper and assign some children a noise. As the orchestra grows, have children hold up their noise cards to remind others which comes next.

Out and In

There were two skunks,
Out and In.
When In was out, Out was in.
One day Out was in
And In was out.

Their mother,
Who was in with Out,
Wanted In in.
"Bring In in,"
She said to Out.

So Out went out
And brought In in.
"How did you find him
So fast?" asked Mother.
"Instinct," he answered.

SUGGESTION: This poem is tricky to read. It helps if students have heard it several times before they see the printed version. Point out quotation marks and commas so that children will comprehend the meaning of the words. It's a perfect poem to revisit as you deal with antonyms.

Over in the Meadow

Over in the meadow,
In the sand in the sun
Lived an old mother toadie
And her little toadie one.
"Wink!" said the mother;
"I wink!" said the one,
So they winked and they blinked
In the sand in the sun.

Over in the meadow,
Where the stream runs blue
Lived an old mother fish
And her little fishes two.
"Swim!" said the mother;
"We swim!" said the two,
So they swam and they leaped
Where the stream runs blue.

Over in the meadow,
In a hole in a tree
Lived an old mother bluebird
And her little birdies three.
"Sing!" said the mother;
"We sing!" said the three
So they sang and were glad
In a hole in the tree.

continued

SUGGESTION: Children may have sung or heard "Over in the Meadow" before but may not have explored all the verses listed here. Children can work as partners to select, learn, illustrate, and read aloud one verse. Their products can be combined to make a class book.

Over in the meadow,
In the reeds on the shore
Lived an old mother muskrat
And her little ratties four.
"Dive!" said the mother;
"We dive!" said the four
So they dived and they burrowed
In the reeds on the shore.

Over in the meadow,
In a snug beehive
Lived a mother honey bee
And her little bees five.
"Buzz!" said the mother;
"We buzz!" said the five
So they buzzed and they hummed
In the snug beehive.

ADDITIONAL VERSES:

Over in the meadow,
In a nest built of sticks
Lived a black mother crow
And her little crows six.
"Caw!" said the mother;
"We caw!" said the six
So they cawed and they called
In their nest built of sticks.

Over in the meadow,
Where the grass is so even
Lived a gay mother cricket
And her little crickets seven.
"Chirp!" said the mother;
"We chirp!" said the seven
So they chirped cheery notes
In the grass soft and even.

Over in the meadow,
By the old mossy gate
Lived a brown mother lizard
And her little lizards eight.
"Bask!" said the mother;
"We bask!" said the eight
So they basked in the sun
On the old mossy gate.

Over in the meadow,
Where the quiet pools shine
Lived a green mother frog
And her little froggies nine.
"Croak!" said the mother;
"We croak!" said the nine
So they croaked and they splashed
Where the quiet pools shine.

Over in the meadow,
In a sly little den
Lived a gray mother spider
And her little spiders ten.
"Spin!" said the mother;
"We spin!" said the ten
So they spun lacy webs
In their sly little den.

Over the River and Through the Wood

by Lydia Marie Child

Over the river and through the wood,
To grandmother's house we go;
The horse knows the way to carry the sleigh,
Through white and drifted snow.
Over the river and through the wood,
Oh, how the wind does blow!
It stings the toes and bites the nose,
As over the fields we go!

Over the river and through the wood,
Trot fast, my dapple gray!
Spring over the ground like a hunting hound,
For this is Thanksgiving Day!
Over the river and through the wood,
Now grandmother's face I spy!
Hurrah for the fun! Is the pudding done?
Hurrah for the pumpkin pie!

SUGGESTION: Teach children this song for the Thanksgiving holiday. Pair the song with the picture book *Over the River and Through the Woods*, illustrated by John Steven Gurney. The illustrations will give students an idea about how this holiday was celebrated and how people lived in other times and places.

Owl

A wise old owl lived in an oak,

The more he saw, the less he spoke.

The less he spoke, the more he heard.

Why can't we all be like that wise old bird?

SUGGESTION: Children need to hear the sounds of many different kinds of poems read aloud. This piece is written to give advice. Help children figure out what that advice is. After children learn this poem, one child may read the last line as a "solo."

Pairs or Pears

Twelve pairs hanging high

Twelve knights riding by

Each knight took a pear,

And yet left a dozen there.

SUGGESTION: Children will enjoy figuring out the riddle of this short rhyme. Having it on chart paper or in a pocket chart may help them compare the homophones for meaning. If they don't notice, be sure to point out the additional four words in the verse that have words that sound the same but are spelled differently *(knight/night; there/their; high/hi; by/bye)*. Give them a photocopy of this verse and ask them to work in groups to create a second verse focusing on the other homophone pairings.

Pawpaw Patch

Where, oh where,
Is dear little Nellie?
Where, oh where,
Is dear little Nellie?
Where, oh where,
Is dear little Nellie?
Way down yonder
In the pawpaw patch.

Come on, boys,
Let's go find her.
Come on, boys,
Let's go find her.
Come on, boys,
Let's go find her.
Way down yonder
In the pawpaw patch.

Picking up pawpaws,
Puttin' 'em in your pocket,
Picking up pawpaws,
Puttin' 'em in your pocket,
Picking up pawpaws,
Puttin' 'em in your pocket,
Way down yonder
In the pawpaw patch.

SUGGESTION: Children will be fascinated with the idea of a *pawpaw patch*. This seemingly nonsense word is actually the name of a type of tree from central and southern United States that produces oblong, yellowish fruit.

A Peanut Sat on a Railroad Track

A peanut sat on a railroad track,

His heart was all a-flutter.

Then 'round the bend came a railroad train.

Toot! Toot! Peanut butter!

Squish!

SUGGESTION: *Toot! Toot!* is just one sound the train can make as it comes down the railroad track. Children can incorporate other sound effects, such as a bell, tambourine, whistle, and even other words, such as *chooo-choo*, *ch-ch-ch-ch*, and *whooo-oo-oo-ooo*. Motions can show a heart *a-flutter* and how the train comes *'round the bend*. For a grand finale, children can mash hands together on *Peanut butter*.

Peter Piper

Peter Piper picked a peck of pickled peppers;

Did Peter Piper pick a peck of pickled peppers?

If Peter Piper picked a peck of pickled peppers,

Where's the peck of pickled peppers

Peter Piper picked?

SUGGESTION: This tongue twister can be read and recited slowly at first and then faster and faster. Consider pairing Peter and Betty (*Peter Piper* and *Betty Botter*) together when reviewing middle consonant sounds represented by double letters. The fun of the tongue twisters will have the children noticing double consonants everywhere. You could also revisit this when children are looking to form past tense by adding *ed*.

Porridge Is Bubbling

Porridge is bubbling, bubbling hot.

Stir it 'round and 'round in the pot,

The bubbles plip,

The bubbles plop.

It's ready to eat all bubbling hot.

Wake up, children.

Wake up soon.

We'll eat the porridge with a spoon.

SUGGESTION: The poem mimicks the sounds of porridge in the words *bubble*, *plip*, and *plop*. Have children think of other words that sound like a real noise.

The Postman

The whistling postman swings along.

His bag is deep and wide,

And messages from all the world

Are bundled up inside.

The postman's walking up our street.

Soon now he'll ring my bell.

Perhaps there'll be a letter stamped

In Asia. Who can tell?

SUGGESTION: Children enjoy sending and receiving mail. You might present this poem at a time when the class has written to someone (or ordered something) and received a reply. Children can also talk about whether they have ever received letters.

The Ptarmigan

The ptarmigan is strange,

As strange as he can be;

Never sits on the ptelephone poles

Or roosts upon a ptree.

And the way he ptakes pto spelling

Is the strangest thing pto me.

SUGGESTION: Help children notice the playful spellings—*ptelephone*, *ptree*, *ptakes*, and *pto*—that emphasize the weird but correctly spelled word *ptarmigan*. Students may use highlighter tape or yellow crayon to mark these words on their own copies of this verse.

fold
here

219

Queen, Queen Caroline

Queen, Queen Caroline,

Dipped her hair in turpentine;

Turpentine made it shine,

Queen, Queen Caroline.

SUGGESTION: Be sure to pronounce Caroline with a long *i* sound to rhyme with turpentine. You may need to explain that turpentine takes paint off and it wouldn't be good to use on your hair, but that it also makes the poem funny. This poem is also good for working with the *i*/consonant/silent *e* pattern.

The Rain

Splish, splash,

Splish, splash,

Drip, drop,

Drip, drop,

Will the rain ever stop?

SUGGESTION: Children can really simulate the sound of the rain when they learn this rhyme and say it as a round. Invite one group to start and the next group to begin when the previous group has finished the second line. Vary the rainstorm by reciting the verse fast, slowly, loudly, softly, and so on.

fold
here

221

The Rain Is Raining All Around

by Robert Louis Stevenson

The rain is raining all around,

It falls on field and tree,

It falls on the umbrellas here,

And on the ships at sea.

SUGGESTION: Children may enjoy making a mural backdrop or series of poetry charts that show the rain coming down in many different places all over the world. Having groups recite the poem—or several rain poems—in front of the charts or mural makes a great performance, integrating several curriculum areas.

River

Runs all day and never walks,

Often murmurs, never talks,

It has a bed but never sleeps,

It has a mouth but never eats.

SUGGESTION: Don't reveal the title of this poem; let your students name the verse themselves after they solve the puzzle. The lines of this riddle will keep them guessing: What it could mean to have a bed but never sleep? They may need help with the word *murmurs*.

fold
here

223

Robert Rowley

Robert Rowley rolled a round roll 'round;

A round roll Robert Rowley rolled 'round.

If Robert Rowley rolled a round roll 'round,

Where rolled the round roll Robert Rowley rolled 'round?

SUGGESTION: This is another tongue twister with very tricky words. Most children love the challenge of saying these kinds of poems faster and faster.

Rock-a-bye Baby

Rock-a-bye baby

In the treetop,

When the wind blows,

The cradle will rock.

When the bough breaks,

The cradle will fall,

And down will come baby,

Cradle and all.

SUGGESTION: All children are familiar with this classic, and it can be fun to revisit when introducing word-solving actions such as connecting words that have the same spelling but different meanings and possibly different sounds (*rock, wind, will, fall, down*).

Row, Row, Row Your Boat

Row, row, row your boat

Gently down the stream;

Merrily, merrily, merrily, merrily,

Life is but a dream.

Row, row, row your boat

Down the jungle stream;

If you see a crocodile,

Don't forget to scream!

Row, row, row your boat

All day in the rain;

Merrily, merrily, merrily, merrily,

You may end up in Spain.

SUGGESTION: Undoubtedly, all the children will have had experience with this song. Sing it as a round after they know it. That makes it a perfect one to revisit, especially when you are working with letter combinations that represent long vowel songs. This song has word examples for *ai*, *ay*, *ee*, *ea*, *oa*, and *ow*.

A Sailor Went to Sea

A sailor went to sea, sea, sea.

To see what he could see, see, see.

But all that he could see, see, see,

Was the bottom of the deep blue sea, sea, sea.

SUGGESTION: This nonsense rhyme calls attention to the homonyms *sea* and *see*. Adding simple hand movements for *sea* (hand shows motion of waves) and *see* (hand over eyes as if blocking sun) helps children distinguish the meaning and spelling differences.

fold
here

227

The Sausage

The sausage is a cunning bird

With feathers long and wavy;

It swims about the frying pan

And makes its nest in gravy.

SUGGESTION: Don't let your class miss the craziness of this image of a *sausage bird* swimming around and nesting in a frying pan. Teach children to notice comparisons in which one thing is used to represent another. (This poem does not say *directly* that a sausage is like a bird, but the comparison is *implied*.) Get children's thoughts about why the poet would compare a sausage to a bird.

Seasons

In the spring, leaves are growing,
Green, green leaves are growing.
In the spring, leaves are growing,
Growing in the trees.

In the summer, leaves are rustling,
Yellow leaves are rustling.
In the summer, leaves are rustling,
Rustling in the trees.

In the autumn, leaves are falling,
Brown, brown, leaves are falling.
In the autumn, leaves are falling,
Falling from the trees.

In the winter leaves are sleeping,
Black, black leaves are sleeping.
In the winter, leaves are sleeping,
Sleeping in the grass.

SUGGESTION: This poem about the seasons is excellent for choral reading. Divide the group into four and have one group practice and read each stanza. They may also decide to create motions that illustrate the meaning of the stanza.

fold
here

229

The Secret

We have a secret, just we three,
The robin, and I, and the sweet cherry tree;
The bird told the tree, and the tree told me,
And nobody knows it but just us three.

But of course the robin knows it best,
Because he built the—I shan't tell the rest;
And laid the four little—somethings—in it;
I'm afraid I shall tell it every minute.

But if the tree and the robin don't peep,
I'll try my best the secret to keep;
Though I know when the little birds fly about
Then the whole secret will be out.

We have a secret, just we three,
The robin, and I, and the sweet cherry tree;
The bird told the tree, and the tree told me,
And nobody knows it but just us three.

SUGGESTION: It strengthens children's auditory processing when they get the chance to hear a poem first, learn it aurally, and later see it in written form. When they do see the written version, they are amazed that they can read it! When saying the poem as a group, invite the children to stop before the last word in each line and have one child read that last word.

Seven Blackbirds in a Tree

Seven blackbirds in a tree,

Count them and see what they be.

One for sorrow,

Two for joy,

Three for a girl,

Four for a boy,

Five for silver,

Six for gold,

Seven for a secret

That's never been told.

SUGGESTION: Create additional lines for eight, nine, ten, eleven, and twelve blackbirds.

fold
here

231

She Sells Seashells

She sells seashells

On the seashore.

The shells that she sells

Are seashells I'm sure.

So if she sells seashells

On the seashore,

I'm sure that the shells

Are seashore shells.

SUGGESTION: This tongue twister is good emphasis for the /s/ and /sh/ sounds. Children may highlight *sh* on their own copies of this poem using yellow crayons or highlighter pens. Use a different color for words beginning with *s*.

Shoo Fly

Shoo fly,

Don't bother me.

Shoo fly,

Don't bother me.

Shoo fly,

Don't bother me.

I belong to somebody.

SUGGESTION: Children are probably already familiar with this simple poem and always enjoy acting it out by swatting everywhere as they say it. For that reason, it is a great one to revisit when you are reviewing *not* contractions.

fold
here

233

Silly Simon

Silly Simon met a pieman,
Going to the fair.
Says Silly Simon to the pieman,
"Let me taste your ware."

Says the pieman to Silly Simon,
"Show me first your penny."
Says Silly Simon to the pieman,
"Indeed I have not any."

Silly Simon went a-fishing,
For to catch a whale.
All the water he had got
Was in his mother's pail.

Silly Simon went to look,
If plums grew on a thistle.
He pricked his fingers very much,
Which made poor Simon whistle.

He went to catch a dicky bird,
And thought he could not fail,
Because he had a little salt,
To put upon its tail.

He went for water with a sieve,
But soon it ran all through;
And now poor Silly Simon
Bids you all adieu.

SUGGESTION: Children may be familiar with Simon—especially the first two verses—and they'll have fun with the tongue-twisting nature of the poem. The other stanzas may be less familiar, and a bit more challenging, but provide word examples for discussion of many principles children will be learning, such as adding *s*, *ed*, and *ing* to form new words *(plums, pricked, fishing)*; words with the *oo* vowel team *(poor, soon)*; recognizing open syllables *(going, water)*; or connecting words that sound the same but look different *(fair, to, poor, pail)*. This is one to revisit often.

Sing Your Way Home

Sing your way home

At the close of the day.

Sing your way home,

Drive the shadows away.

Smile every mile

For wherever you roam

It will brighten your road,

It will lighten your load,

If you sing your way home.

SUGGESTION: Have children discuss how singing sometimes makes you feel better or makes jobs easier to do. Explain that *brighten your road* and *lighten your load* probably don't mean that you can really see better or help you carry less but does mean that while you are singing, you feel better.

fold
here

235

Sippity Sup

Sippity sup, sippity sup,

Bread and milk from a china cup.

Bread and milk from a bright silver spoon

Made of a piece of the bright silver moon.

Sippity sup, sippity sup,

Sippity, sippity sup.

SUGGESTION: Have the children accompany the words *sippity sup* with some simple instruments.

Skip to My Lou

Chorus

    Skip, skip, skip to my Lou,

    Skip, skip, skip to my Lou,

    Skip, skip, skip to my Lou,

    Skip to my Lou, my dar-lin'.

Fly's in the buttermilk,

Shoo, fly, shoo,

Fly's in the buttermilk,

Shoo, fly, shoo,

Fly's in the buttermilk,

Shoo, fly, shoo,

Skip to my Lou, my dar-lin'.

Chorus

Cows in the cornfield,

What'll I do?

Cows in the cornfield,

What'll I do?

Cows in the cornfield,

What'll I do?

Skip to my Lou, my dar-lin'.

Chorus

continued

SUGGESTION: This song is really a lot of fun to sing and skip to. Have the children form a circle and hold hands. As they sing the song, have them alternate skipping to the left and to the right on each chorus. Pair this poem with the picture book *Cows in the Kitchen*, by June Crebbin.

There's a little red wagon,
Paint it blue,
There's a little red wagon,
Paint it blue,
There's a little red wagon,
Paint it blue,
Skip to my Lou, my dar-lin'.

Chorus

Lost my partner,
What'll I do?
Lost my partner,
What'll I do?
Lost my partner,
What'll I do?
Skip to my Lou, my dar-lin'.

Chorus

I'll find another one,
Prettier than you,
I'll find another one,
Prettier than you,
I'll find another one,
Prettier than you,
Skip to my Lou, my dar-lin'.

continued

Can't get a red bird,
Blue bird'll do,
Can't get a red bird,
Blue bird'll do,
Can't get a red bird,
Blue bird'll do,
Skip to my Lou, my dar-lin'.

Chorus

Cat's in the cream jar,
Ooh, ooh, ooh,
Cat's in the cream jar,
Ooh, ooh, ooh,
Cat's in the cream jar,
Ooh, ooh, ooh,
Skip to my Lou, my dar-lin'.

Chorus

Off to Texas,
Two by two,
Off to Texas,
Two by two,
Off to Texas,
Two by two,
Skip to my Lou, my dar-lin'.

Slowly, Slowly

Slowly, slowly, very slowly

Creeps the garden snail;

Slowly, slowly, very slowly

Up the wooden rail.

SUGGESTION: Children enjoy saying this poem s-l-o-w-l-y, to match the pace of a garden snail.

Sneeze on Monday

Sneeze on Monday, sneeze for danger;

Sneeze on Tuesday, kiss a stranger;

Sneeze on Wednesday, receive a letter;

Sneeze on Thursday, something better;

Sneeze on Friday, expect sorrow;

Sneeze on Saturday, joy tomorrow.

SUGGESTION: Children will be interested to know that the lines of this poem represent what some people used to believe—that sneezes predicted what would happen. They can talk about what we now know about sneezes. After children know the poem, you can revisit it to look at *er* endings or double consonants.

fold
here

241

Snow

by Issa

I could eat it!

This snow that falls

So softly, so softly.

SUGGESTION: This Haiku poem has sensory images in it. Children can talk about the softness of the snow. If you live in a cold climate, this is a good poem to place in a window on a snowy day. Children will notice that the poem does not rhyme.

Snowman

I made a little snowman,

I made him big and round.

I made him from a snowball,

I rolled upon the ground.

He has two eyes, a nose, a mouth,

A lovely scarf of red.

He even has some buttons,

And a hat upon his head.

Melt, melt, melt, melt,

Melt, melt, melt, melt.

SUGGESTION: Divide the group into two or three smaller groups and read the lines alternately at a good pace. Children may want to let their voices diminish over the last two lines, saying the last *melt* in a whisper. Some children may volunteer to draw the snowman in eight frames, each one "melting" a little bit until the last frame just has a puddle and the snowman's eyes, etc. Creating these frames will take some planning.

Someone

by Walter de la Mare

Someone came knocking
At my wee, small door;
Someone came knocking,
I'm sure, sure, sure;
I listened, I opened,
I looked to left and right,
But nought there was a-stirring
In the still dark night;
Only the busy beetle
Tap-tapping in the wall,
Only from the forest
The screech owl's call,
Only the cricket whistling
While the dewdrops fall,
So I know not who came knocking,
At all, at all, at all.

SUGGESTION: Mood is important as this poem is recited. Children's voices can convey the mystery, awe, and downright spookiness of an unknown creature and the *wee, small door.*

Someone's Birthday

Today is a birthday,

I wonder for whom.

We know it's somebody

Who's right in this room.

So look all around you

For somebody who

Is laughing and smiling

My goodness—it's you!

SUGGESTION: After reading the poem, place a special hat or button on the child whose birthday it is. Invite the birthday child to choose a story for the group read-aloud.

fold here

245

Spread It Thick

Yellow butter, purple jelly, red jam, black bread.

Spread it thick, say it quick!

Yellow butter, purple jelly, red jam, black bread.

Spread it thicker, say it quicker!

Yellow butter, purple jelly, red jam, black bread.

Don't eat with your mouth full!

SUGGESTION: Children will enjoy thinking about how this sandwich would look. They may want to substitute other colors for the jelly, jam, and bread. They may not have seen black bread but remind them to look at the colors of bread if they go to the grocery store.

Spring Is Coming

Spring is coming, spring is coming!

How do you think I know?

I see a flower blooming,

I know it must be so.

Spring is coming, spring is coming!

How do you think I know?

I see a blossom on the tree,

I know it must be so.

SUGGESTION: Brainstorm other signs of spring. Write these ideas interactively, sharing the pen with your class. Invite your student poets to read back their wondrous words together and illustrate them. You may want to use this poem in a pocket chart. After developing your list of other signs of spring, help children substitute their ideas *(I see . . .)* for the third line of the pattern.

fold
here

(247)

The Squirrel

Whisky, frisky,

Hippety hop,

Up he scrambles

To the treetop.

Whirly, furly,

What a tail!

Tall as a feather,

Broad as a sail!

Where's his supper?

In the shell.

Snappity, crackity—

Out it fell!

SUGGESTION: Invite children to pick out their favorite descriptive words from the poem, such as *whisky, frisky, whirly, furly, snappity, crackity,* and play with altering their voice—high or low pitched, softer or louder.

Star Light, Star Bright

Star light, star bright,

First star I see tonight.

I wish I may, I wish I might

Have this wish I wish tonight.

Star sight, star height,

Second star I see in flight.

I wish this wish with all delight

I wish this wish to be alright.

SUGGESTION: You can start reciting this poem and children will automatically join in by the end of the first line. They may not have heard the second verse, but it can serve as an introduction or review for working with more difficult phonograms (-*ight*). It can be used as a model for making connections between the parts of known words and the new words they are trying to solve.

Stepping Stones

Stepping over stepping stones, one, two, three,

Stepping over stepping stones, come with me.

The river's very fast,

And the river's very wide,

And we'll step across on stepping stones

And reach the other side.

SUGGESTION: Help your class imagine *stepping stones* and step carefully on them as they recite the poem. This is a great poem to use outdoors on the playground also (with chalk-drawn *river* and *stones*).

Susie Moriar

This is the story of Susie Moriar.
It started one night as Susie sat by the _____.
The fire was so hot,
Susie jumped in a _____.
The pot was so low,
Susie fell in the _____.
The snow was so white,
Susie stayed there all _____.
The night was so long,
Susie sang a love _____.
The song was so sweet,
Susie ran down the _____.
The street was so brown,
Susie ran through the _____.
The town was so big,
Susie jumped on a _____.
The pig jumped so high,
Susie was thrown into the _____.
She couldn't get higher,
But oh! What a ride
Had Susie _____.

SUGGESTION: Have the children fill in the missing word. (The next line starts with the word that is missing at the end of the previous line.) Invite the children to create a new story of Susie Moriar (or another character) with the same structure.

fold
here

251

The Swing

by Robert Louis Stevenson

How do you like to go up in a swing,

Up in the air so blue?

Oh, I do think it the pleasantest thing

Ever a child can do!

Up in the air and over the wall,

Till I can see so wide,

Rivers and trees and cattle and all

Over the countryside—

Till I look down on the garden green,

Down on the roof so brown—

Up in the air I go flying again,

Up in the air and down!

SUGGESTION: Help children think about the things they can see from a swing. The rhythm of this poem is like a swing. Prompt children to think about it when swinging on the playground. Children can think of other ways to take a ride and get an aerial view of things: airplane, helicopter, parachute, spaceship, Ferris wheel, and so forth.

Take Me Out to the Ball Game

Take me out to the ball game,

Take me out with the crowd.

Buy me some peanuts and Cracker Jack,

I don't care if I ever get back.

And it's root, root, root for the home team,

If they don't win it's a shame.

For it's one, two, three strikes, "You're out!"

At the old ball game.

SUGGESTION: Have the children sing the rhyme. Assign a "soloist" to shout *You're out!* and accompany the three strikes with a rhythm instrument.

fold
here

253

Taking Off

The airplane taxis down the field

And heads into the breeze,

It lifts its wheels above the ground,

It skims above the trees,

It rises high and higher

Away up toward the sun,

It's just a speck against the sky

—And now it's gone!

SUGGESTION: For just a few minutes, as they recite this poem, children can get a sense of what it must be like to taxi down a field and take off above the ground, heading toward the sun. This poem may begin in a whisper, be spoken faster and louder as the plane takes off, and taper back to a whisper at the end.

Teacher, Teacher

Teacher, teacher, made a mistake.

She sat down on a chocolate cake.

The cake was soft; teacher fell off.

Teacher, teacher, made a mistake.

SUGGESTION: Children may substitute other words for *teacher* and other flavors for *chocolate*. The versions of this humorous poem can go on and on. You can use it as a circle game in which children say the verse about the next child as you go around.

Terrific Toes

I have such terrific toes.

I take them with me wherever I goes.

I have such fantastic feet.

No matter what, they still smell sweet.

Toes and feet and feet and toes.

There's nothing else as fine as those.

SUGGESTION: Children can perform it expressively. They may want to talk about how the second line sounds funny because *go* has been changed to *goes* to rhyme with *toes*. They may find it interesting to look at the spelling of *toes*, *goes*, and *those*.

There Was a Bee-eye-ee-eye-ee

There was a bee-eye-ee-eye-ee
Sat on a wall-eye-all-eye-all.
And there it sat-eye-at-eye-at
And that was all-eye-all-eye-all.

Then came a boy-eye-oy-eye-oy
Who had a stick-eye-ick-eye-ick.
And gave that bee-eye-ee-eye-ee
An awful lick-eye-ick-eye-ick.

And so that bee-eye-ee-eye-ee
Began to sting-eye-ing-eye-ing.
And hurt that boy-eye-oy-eye-oy
Like anything-eye-ing-eye-ing!

And then that bee-eye-ee-eye-ee
Gave one big cough-eye-ough-eye-ough.
And one last smile-eye-ile-eye-ile
And he buzzed off-eye-off-eye-off.

SUGGESTION: When children have figured out the pattern behind these nonsense words, they will be able to not only read these lines but also feel as if they are speaking another language! Recite the first verse using the echo technique: say a line, pointing to yourself; then gesture toward the children and invite them to say the line with you. Say the poem several times this way until the children are comfortable saying it and want to say it on their own. Invite children to use stick-on highlighter tape (in transparent colors) to emphasize the nonsense word patterns.

There Was a Crooked Man

There was a crooked man

Who walked a crooked mile.

He found a crooked sixpence

Against a crooked stile.

He bought a crooked cat,

Which caught a crooked mouse.

And they all lived together

In a little crooked house.

SUGGESTION: Everything is crooked in this nursery rhyme! You can have fun with the language by substituting *crooked* for words such as *wicked* or other suggestions children offer. Children love creating all these crooked details for a mural or poetry chart.

There Was a Little Girl

by Henry Wadsworth Longfellow

There was a little girl

Who had a little curl

Right in the middle of her forehead.

When she was good

She was very, very good,

But when she was bad she was horrid.

SUGGESTION: Have children share ways they have been good, bad, and horrid. Ask them to think of other words that mean the same as *horrid*, for example, *terrible, naughty, horrible, rude.*

fold
here

259

There Was a Little Turtle

by Rachel Lindsay

There was a little turtle.

He lived in a box.

He swam in a puddle.

He climbed on the rocks.

He snapped at a mosquito.

He snapped at a flea.

He snapped at a minnow.

He snapped at me.

He caught the mosquito.

He caught the flea.

He caught the minnow.

But . . . he didn't catch me!

SUGGESTION: Invite all the children to read the first verse, have half of them read the second verse, have the other half read the third verse, and have everyone read the last line. This poem is infectious. Children love to recite it and mime the turtle's motions.

There Was an Old Man of Blackheath

There was an old man of Blackheath

Who sat on his set of false teeth.

Said he, with a start,

"Oh dear, bless my heart!

I've bitten myself underneath!"

SUGGESTION: This is another limerick that can be compared with "The Old Man and the Cow" and several other limericks in this book. After children have read quite a few limericks, they can begin to make their own. Consider making a class book of limericks.

fold
here

261

There Was an Old Man of Dumbree

by Edward Lear

There was an Old Man of Dumbree,

Who taught little Owls to drink Tea;

For he said, "To eat mice

Is not proper or nice,"

That amiable Man of Dumbree.

SUGGESTION: This limerick can be added to a class book of limericks. Children will enjoy the idea of eating mice.

There Was an Old Man With a Beard

by Edward Lear

There was an old man with a beard,

Who said, "It is just as I feared!

Two owls and a hen,

Four larks and a wren,

Have all built their nests in my beard!"

SUGGESTION: Children will like acting out this poem as well as illustrating it. This would be a good choice for a poetry performance incorporating several poems: students could take turns acting out and reciting "There Was an Old Man With a Beard," "Dr. Foster," "Peter Piper," and "Mr. Nobody," for example.

There Was an Old Person of Ware

by Edward Lear

There was an old person of Ware,

Who rode on the back of a bear.

When they asked, "Does it trot?"

He said, "Certainly not!

He's a Moppsikon Floppsikon bear!"

SUGGESTION: Assign two children to read the dialogue.

There Was an Old Woman

There was an old woman tossed up in a basket,

Seventeen times as high as the moon.

And where was she going, I couldn't but ask it.

For in her hand she carried a broom.

"Old woman, old woman, old woman," said I,

"Oh whither, oh whither, oh whither so high?"

"To sweep the cobwebs off the sky."

"Shall I go with you?"

"Aye, by and by."

SUGGESTION: Children can appreciate the imagination in this poem—an old woman in the sky sweeping cobwebs. Have them talk about what the cobwebs might be. Ask children to think about what *whither* might mean ("where").

fold
here

265

There Was a Small Maiden Named Maggie

There was a small maiden named Maggie,

Whose dog was enormous and shaggy;

The front end of him

Looked vicious and grim—

But the tail end was friendly and waggy.

SUGGESTION: All kinds of variations of this limerick can be created by finding substitutes for *small, maiden*, and *Maggie*. The dog is the main point of interest. Invite children to draw a dog that looks *vicious* and *friendly, enormous* and *shaggy*.

There Was a Young Farmer
of Leeds

There was a young farmer of Leeds

Who swallowed six packets of seeds.

It soon came to pass

He was covered with grass,

And he couldn't sit down for the weeds.

SUGGESTION: This limerick has a humorous ending and may be fun to draw in a sequence of cartoon panels. Have the children stop before each rhyming word at the end of the line and invite a "soloist" to read it.

fold
here

267

There Was a Young Lad of St. Just

There was a young lad of St. Just

Who ate apple pie till he bust;

It wasn't the fru-it

That caused him to do it,

What finished him off was the crust.

SUGGESTION: This limerick follows the familiar structure. Children may want to talk about how the word *fruit* had to be structured as *fru-it* to make the rhyme work.

There's a Hole in the Bucket

There's a hole in the bucket, dear Liza, dear Liza,
There's a hole in the bucket, dear Liza, a hole.

Well, fix it, dear Henry, dear Henry, dear Henry,
Well, fix it, dear Henry, dear Henry, fix it.

With what shall I fix it, dear Liza, dear Liza,
With what shall I fix it, dear Liza, with what?

With a straw, dear Henry, dear Henry, dear Henry,
With a straw, dear Henry, dear Henry, with a straw.

But the straw is too long, dear Liza, dear Liza,
But the straw is too long, dear Liza, too long.

Then cut it, dear Henry, dear Henry, dear Henry,
Then cut it, dear Henry, dear Henry, then cut it.

Well, how shall I cut it, dear Liza, dear Liza,
Well, how shall I cut it, dear Liza, well how?

With an axe, dear Henry, dear Henry, dear Henry,
With an axe, dear Henry, dear Henry, with an axe.

But the axe is too dull, dear Liza, dear Liza,
But the axe is too dull, dear Liza, too dull.

Then sharpen it, dear Henry, dear Henry, dear Henry,
Then sharpen it, dear Henry, dear Henry, then sharpen it.

On what shall I sharpen it, dear Liza, dear Liza,
On what shall I sharpen it, dear Liza, on what? *continued*

SUGGESTION: Children can sing the song together; then substitute names of children in the class. For more emphasis, ask them to say, rather than sing, the last two lines.

On a stone, dear Henry, dear Henry, dear Henry,
On a stone, dear Henry, dear Henry, on a stone.

But the stone is too dry, dear Liza, dear Liza,
But the stone is too dry, dear Liza, too dry.

Then wet it, dear Henry, dear Henry, dear Henry,
Then wet it, dear Henry, dear Henry, then wet it.

With what shall I wet it, dear Liza, dear Liza,
With what shall I wet it, dear Liza, with what?

With water, dear Henry, dear Henry, dear Henry,
With water, dear Henry, dear Henry, with water.

Well, how shall I carry it, dear Liza, dear Liza,
Well, how shall I carry it, dear Liza, well how?

In a bucket, dear Henry, dear Henry, dear Henry,
In a bucket, dear Henry, dear Henry, in a bucket.

BUT THERE'S A HOLE IN THE BUCKET,
    DEAR LIZA, DEAR LIZA,
THERE'S A HOLE IN THE BUCKET, DEAR LIZA, A HOLE.

They That Wash on Monday

They that wash on Monday,

Have all the week to dry.

They that wash on Tuesday,

Are not so much awry.

They that wash on Wednesday,

Are not so much to blame.

They that wash on Thursday,

Wash for very shame.

They that wash on Friday,

Wash in sorry need.

They that wash on Saturday,

Are lazy folk indeed.

SUGGESTION: Partners will enjoy getting a chance to read this poem together, alternating each pair of lines. If you perform it as a class, one student "soloist" can read the names of days of the week. Children will also have many ideas for writing their own versions of things to do on different days of the week.

Thirty Days Has September

Thirty days has September,

April, June, and November.

February has twenty-eight alone.

All the rest have thirty-one.

Excepting leap year, that's the time,

When February's days are twenty-nine.

SUGGESTION: This is a handy poem for children to know throughout their lives as they deal with calendars. When this information about the number of days in each month is committed to memory in verse form, it is easy to recall.

A Thunderstorm

Boom, bang, boom, bang,

Rumpety, lumpety, bump!

Zoom, zam, zoom, zam,

Clippity, clappity, clump!

Rustles and bustles

And swishes and zings!

What wonderful sounds

A thunderstorm brings.

SUGGESTION: This verse is a great opportunity for children to find everyday objects and simple rhythm instruments to use to make a thunderstorm: bells, wooden sticks, a xylophone, tambourines, rain sticks. Invite children to talk about the words in the poem that make them think of real sounds in a thunderstorm. You might want to pair this with "I Hear Thunder" (also in this volume).

fold
here

273

Tree Shadows

All hushed the trees are waiting

On tiptoe for the sight

Of moonrise shedding splendor

Across the dusk of night.

Ah, now the moon is risen

And lo, without a sound,

The trees all write their welcome

Far along the ground!

SUGGESTION: Invite children to visualize this scene and recite the poem softly. One or more children may add background sounds, such as brushing the mallet across the keys of a xylophone. Let children take the lead in deciding what sounds to create.

Tumbling

In jumping and tumbling

We spend the whole day,

Till night by arriving

Has finished our play.

What then? One and all,

There's no more to be said,

As we tumbled all day,

So we tumble to bed.

SUGGESTION: Children may want to make tumbling and jumping hand motions while reciting this poem; the last line may be read very slowly, as tired children *tumble to bed*.

fold here

275

The Turtle

The turtle crawls on the ground

And makes a loud rustling sound.

He carries his house wherever he goes,

And when he is scared,

He pulls in his nose and covers his toes!

SUGGESTION: As children recite and read the poem, they will enjoy making their voices stretch out the words slowly, just the way a turtle gets around. To capture the excitement of the last line, have the children read it quickly and loudly.

The Tutor

A tutor who tooted the flute

Tried to tutor two tooters to toot.

Said the two to the tutor,

"Is it harder to toot, or

To tutor two tooters to toot?"

SUGGESTION: The words to this quick tongue twister are almost musical. Children love *tooting* their way through the words using a kazoo. Half may *toot* quietly while the rest recite.

Two in the Middle

Two in the middle and two at the end,

Each is a sister and each is a friend.

A penny to save and a penny to spend,

Two in the middle and two at the end.

SUGGESTION: This poem has a contagious rhythm. Children may wish to draw this poem to help them figure it out.

Two Little Feet

Two little feet go tap, tap, tap.

Two little hands go clap, clap, clap.

A quiet little leap up from my chair.

Two little arms reach up in the air.

Two little feet go jump, jump, jump.

Two little fists go thump, thump, thump.

One little body goes round, round, round.

And one little child sits quietly down.

SUGGESTION: This poem can be introduced and used as a transition for children to move from one activity to another, or as a signal for gathering on the rug. The repetitive movements engage the children while allowing them an opportunity to make this an energetic physical, as well as an oral language, activity. Also notice that this verse provides several examples of words in which *y* makes a vowel sound. Revisit this fun verse when children are working with that principle.

fold
here

Two Little Kittens

Two little kittens, one stormy night,
Began to quarrel and then to fight.
One had a mouse, the other had none,
And that's the way the quarrel's begun.

"I'll have that mouse," said the biggest cat.
"You'll have that mouse? We'll see about that!"
"I *will* have that mouse," said the eldest son.
"You *shan't* have the mouse," said the little one.

I told you before 'twas a stormy night,
When these two little kittens began to fight.
The old woman seized her sweeping broom,
And swept the two kittens right out of the room.

The ground was covered with frost and snow,
And the two little kittens had nowhere to go.
So they laid them down on the mat at the door,
While the old woman finished sweeping the floor.

Then they crept in, as quiet as mice,
All wet with the snow and as cold as ice.
For they found it was better, that stormy night,
To lie down and sleep than to quarrel and fight.

SUGGESTION: When children know this poem, they will be able to read it easily from a pocket chart, overhead transparency, or poetry chart. They may enjoy playing with the language and acting out the parts of the biggest cat and the little one.

Two Times Table

Twice one are two,

Violets white and blue.

Twice two are four,

Sunflowers at the door.

Twice three are six,

Sweet peas on their sticks.

Twice four are eight,

Poppies at the gate.

Twice five are ten,

Pansies bloom again.

ADDITIONAL VERSES:

Twice six are twelve,
Pinks for those who delve.

Twice seven are fourteen,
Flowers of the runner bean.

Twice eight are sixteen,
Clinging ivy ever green.

Twice nine are eighteen,
Purple thistles to be seen.

Twice ten are twenty,
Hollyhocks in plenty.

Twice eleven are twenty-two,
Daisies wet with morning dew.

Twice twelve are twenty-four,
Roses . . . who could ask for more.

SUGGESTION: This poem focuses on multiplying by two, so you will not want to use it until you are teaching children multiplication. For each number, flowers/plants are mentioned in the second line, ending with roses. Children can read the poem but also look at a mathematical equation; they can create the drawings that represent the answers to the equations.

2 Y's

2 Y's U R.

2 Y's U B.

I C U R

2 Y's 4 me!

SUGGESTION: Understanding this poem will require reading it aloud. Have children, in partners, read the poem aloud to each other. Then have the whole group talk about how the names of numbers and letters have been used to create the meaning of the poem. End by reading the poem together. Children may like to follow up by creating messages using numbers and letters.

A Twister of Twists

A twister of twists once twisted a twist.

The twist that he twisted was a three-twisted twist;

If in twisting the twist, one twist should untwist,

The untwisted twist would untwist the twist.

SUGGESTION: This verse is quite a tongue twister. If students hear this first and then read it slowly, they will find it easier to speed up and say the words quickly. This is an enjoyable challenge and helps develop articulation.

fold
here

283

Up in the North

Up in the north a long way off,

A donkey caught the whooping cough.

What shall we give him to make him better?

Salt, mustard, vinegar, and pepper.

Up in the north a long way off,

The donkey's got the whooping cough.

He whooped so hard with the whooping cough,

He whooped his head and his tail right off.

SUGGESTION: The poem gives us a crazy and humorous visual image: a donkey with the whooping cough, trying all kinds of remedies, as his head and tail "whoop" off. Children will love racing through to the end of the poem just to get to say the last two lines.

Walk Fast

Walk fast in snow,

In frost walk slow,

And still as you go,

Tread on your toe.

When frost and snow are both together,

Sit by the fire and spare shoe leather.

SUGGESTION: Children can talk about walking in winter weather. If you are in a cold climate, they may have boots and can talk about how snow, ice, frost, or rain is hard on shoes. They can discuss the overall meaning of the poem—stay in during really cold weather!

fold
here

285

A Walk One Day

When I went out for a walk one day

My head fell off and rolled away,

And when I saw that it was gone,

I picked it up and put it on.

When I went out into the street

Someone shouted, "Look at your feet."

I looked at them and sadly said,

"I've left them both asleep in bed."

SUGGESTION: After students have learned this poem, they may wish to present it as a play, one child enacting each stanza. Or one group can say the poem while another group does an eerie, whispered chorus for each verse: "Where is your head? Where is your head?" and "Look at your feet. Look at your feet."

Walking Through the Jungle

Walking through the jungle,
What do you see?
Can you hear a noise?
What could it be?

Ah well, I think it is a snake, Sss! Sss! Sss!
I think it is a snake, Sss! Sss! Sss!
I think it is a snake, Sss! Sss! Sss!
Looking for his tea.

Walking through the jungle,
What do you see?
Can you hear a noise?
What could it be?

Ah well, I think it is a tiger, Roar! Roar! Roar!
I think it is a tiger, Roar! Roar! Roar!
I think it is a tiger, Roar! Roar! Roar!
Looking for his tea.

Walking through the jungle,
What do you see?
Can you hear a noise?
What could it be?

Ah well, I think it is a crocodile, Snap! Snap! Snap!
I think it is a crocodile, Snap! Snap! Snap!
I think it is a crocodile, Snap! Snap! Snap!
Looking for his tea.
HOPE IT ISN'T ME!

SUGGESTION: After children are familiar with the words and structure (a pocket chart version is helpful), ask them to come up with other animals and sounds to create new verses.

Wash the Dishes

Wash the dishes,

Wipe the dishes,

Ring the bell for tea.

Three good wishes,

Three good kisses,

I will give to thee.

SUGGESTION: Children love to mime the actions and numbers given in the lines of this verse. Its simple structure and examples make it perfect to revisit when working on forming plurals by adding *es* to words.

What Is Pink?

by Christina Rossetti

What is pink? A rose is pink
By the fountain's brink.

What is red? A poppy's red
In its barley bed.

What is blue? The sky is blue
Where the clouds float through.

What is white? A swan is white
Sailing in the night.

What is yellow? Pears are yellow,
Rich and ripe and mellow.

What is green? The grass is green,
With small flowers between.

What is violet? Clouds are violet
In the summer twilight.

What is orange? Why, an orange,
Just an orange!

SUGGESTION: Christina Rossetti's poem pairs colors with specially chosen items. Ask your students what things they associate with specific colors. Invite them to write their own short poems pairing a color with something special to them.

When I Was One

When I was one I ate a bun
The day I went to sea;
I jumped aboard a sailing ship
And the captain said to me:
"We're going this way, that way,
Forward and backward, over the deep blue sea.
A bright yellow sun and lots of fun
And that's the life for me."

When I was two I buckled my shoe
The day I went to sea;
I jumped aboard a sailing ship
And the captain said to me:
"We're going this way, that way,
Forward and backward, over the deep blue sea.
A bright yellow sun and lots of fun
And that's the life for me."

ADDITIONAL VERSES:
When I was three I hurt my knee . . .
When I was four I fell on the floor . . .
When I was five I learned to dive . . .
When I was six the sail I did fix . . .

SUGGESTION: This poem has the rhythm of a sailor's chanty. Tell children about the days of tall clipper ships when sailors sang chantys as they worked. As children recite the poem, they can sway like ocean waves, forward and backward as the captain directs. Children like to take turns being the captain of the ship.

Where Go the Boats?

by Robert Louis Stevenson

Dark brown is the river,
Golden is the sand.
It flows along forever,
With trees on either hand.

Green leaves a-floating,
Castles of the foam,
Boats of mine a-boating—
Where will all come home?

On goes the river
And out past the mill,
Away down the valley,
Away down the hill.

Away down the river,
A hundred miles or more,
Other little children
Shall bring my boats ashore.

SUGGESTION: Be sure to share this as a read-aloud several times to emphasize the poetic language. This poem may be rewritten as a class book or individual booklet, with a page for each stanza. Use with the picture book *Where Go the Boats: Play-Poems of Robert Louis Stevenson*, illustrated by Max Grover. The poetic language of this poem also provides many word examples of vowel combinations (*ay, oa, ee, ea, ow*). Plan to revisit this poem when children are working on recognizing and using letter combinations that represent long vowel sounds.

fold here

291

Whether the Weather

Whether the weather be fine

Or whether the weather be not.

Whether the weather be cold.

Or whether the weather be hot.

We'll weather the weather

Whether we like it or not!

SUGGESTION: Help children talk about the double meaning of *weather* in the poem. After children know the poem, you can contrast the words *whether* and *weather*, which in some parts of the United States sound exactly alike and in others sound different (the *wh* being a soft sound with air blown out and the *w* being harder with no breath).

Whistle

"Whistle, daughter, whistle,

Whistle, daughter, dear."

"I cannot whistle, mommy,

I cannot whistle clear."

"Whistle, daughter, whistle,

Whistle all around."

"I cannot whistle, mommy,

I cannot make a sound."

SUGGESTION: Children may identify with either being able to whistle or not. Once children know and can read the poem, you may want to revisit it to look at vowel pairs such as *au*, *ea*, *ou*.

Who Has Seen the Wind?

by Christina Rossetti

Who has seen the wind?

Neither I nor you:

But when the leaves hang trembling

The wind is passing through.

Who has seen the wind?

Neither you nor I:

But when the trees bow down their heads

The wind is passing by.

SUGGESTION: Have children find a way to move to enact the wind as they recite this poem. Have one group do movements while other groups say the words of the poem or make various wind noises. The poem is full of visual images that children can discuss and appreciate.

The Wind

Swoosh, swirl,

Swoosh, swirl,

Watch the leaves

Tumble and twirl.

SUGGESTION: Children will love to *swoosh* and *swirl* as they recite this poem. Afterward, ask them to talk about how the words of the poem help them see the motion of the leaves.

The Wind Blows High

The wind,

The wind,

The wind blows high.

The rain,

The rain,

Scatters down the sky.

SUGGESTION: Invite children to think about the images in this poem and to discuss how to say it. The poem could be said in a very measured way for the first five lines and then in a quicker and descending voice for the last line. They may use some motions—hands high and swooping for the wind and then moving quickly down to simulate rain. They can make their own poems using other weather concepts—clouds, hail.

The Zigzag Boy and Girl

I know a little zigzag boy

Who goes this way and that.

He never knows just where he put

His coat or shoes or hat.

I know a little zigzag girl

Who flutters here and there.

She never knows just where to find

Her brush to fix her hair.

If you are not a zigzag child,

You'll have no cause to say

That you forgot, for you will know

Where things are put away.

SUGGESTION: Everyone will vie to explain and act out the word *zigzag*. Some children wear zigzag parts in their hair. What other zigzags can be found in the classroom or school environment?

fold
here

297